FROM TEA TO COFFEE

The Journey of an "Educated Youth"

Cheng Wang

Published by Open Books

Copyright © 2021 by Cheng Wang

Interior design by Siva Ram Maganti

Cover images ©luts777 shutterstock.com/g/luts777 and ©Glitter-studio shutterstock.com/g/Glitterstudio

ISBN-13: 978-1948598514

Praise for *From Tea to Coffee*

"Cheng Wang's transformative evolution from young Communist ideologue to astute western observer is a must-read cultural travelogue. His deeply personal story provides remarkable insight into the unique diversity of Chinese and American attitudes and divisions."

—Don Vaughan, founder,
Triangle Association of Freelancers, North Carolina

"*From Tea to Coffee* is a life journey of powerful personal transformation. Author, Cheng Wang, shares a glimpse into the cultural drama of struggle and triumph from Mao's time in China to the present-day U.S.A. From an "educated youth" with almost no education in the Mao era to becoming a Ph.D. Candidate at the University of Cincinnati and with no English writing education to becoming a published author, Cheng proves that anyone can persevere and overcome whatever obstacles that may stand in your way."

— Michelle Prince, Best-Selling Author, Performance Publishing Group www.PerformancePublishingGroup.com

"*From Tea to Coffee* is a wonderful exploration of history and a life that has extended across half a century and two continents. For those who believe that East and West can never meet or can only stand in opposition to each other, this memoir offers a beautiful counterpoint. In it we see a clear example of how the two cultures can complement each other perfectly."

—Bennett R. Coles, award-winning author of six published books including *Dark Star Rising*

"From working in the field to published author, Cheng Wang shares how he developed his sense of self. He reshaped himself as he broke through barrier after barrier, driving himself to personal improvement and success."

—Deanna Martinez-Bey,
Social media manager, copy editor, and ten-time author

This book is dedicated to China's lost generation,
whose voices are forever missing.

INTRODUCTION

CHANCES ARE, YOU HAVE never heard the name Cheng Wang—not as an author, anyway. Even those who have known me my entire life have never thought of me in that way. It can be easy to assume that memoir writing is a privilege for celebrities. So, in a culture of 'go big or go home,' who would care to read an account by someone like me—and when written in my second language, no less?

Although I had met inquisitive eyes when I found myself as the only Chinese face among American tennis friends, writer friends, comedy club buddies, and acquaintances at writers' conferences or workshops, I usually touched on my past as a "sent-down youth" in China in casual chats. Many expressed interest in how I later started a new life in America with nothing but $200.00 and a dream, and how I currently call both sides of the Pacific my home, but I never seriously thought of putting it down in a book.

Until one day, I realized that my coming of age in China, followed by my emerging adulthood in America, was not my personal tale, but rather a generational trauma and revival.

For those in our generation, history betrayed our youthful zeal. According to Chinese data, sixteen million "Educated Youths" were sent to the countryside for re-education during those years. As a result, more than a generation of talented people has been deprived of formal education; thus, their voices are forever missing. Only a handful of them have transcended the socioeconomic and cultural barriers that stand between them and the rest of the world.

Be it by fate or personality, I am one of those fortunate few, which obliges me to get our story out. Otherwise, our past will have been effectively written off: like a tree that falls in a forest with no one around to hear it. Therefore, this story demanded to be told.

Fired by this sense of mission, I decided to write a book. But where, then, to begin? All the people and events had faded into distant memory. And the social, cultural, and political backdrop of my early years is so obscure and bizarre, even in the eyes of present-day Chinese. Could it reach Western readers?

Then, in September 2019, I stumbled upon an online writing course: Memoir and Personal Essay Writing. In one assignment, I wrote two pages entitled: "Heavenly Happiness," which is the direct translation of TianXi, where I was sent for re-education.

The best part of this course was the peer reviews. About 100 students took this course at different paces; many introduced themselves as journalists, reporters, or aspiring authors who wanted to learn memoir writing. For the next nine months, I received feedback from aspiring and professional writers taking the same class. Their verdict was unanimous: "Heavenly Happiness" was fascinating precisely because of the differences in time and culture.

Their enthusiasms fueled my desires and convinced me that our early, peculiar past had contemporary value. After much thought, I recognized that this part of history is still at play in many ways. The decade-long Cultural Revolution scarred us, and the repercussions of that have passed through generations into the present day. Most people, including many current leaders in China, were directly affected by those years. Xi Jinping (President of the People's Republic of China since 2013) was an Educated Youth. At age fifteen, he was sent to Liangjiahe Village on the Loess Plateau, one of the most impoverished regions in northwestern China in 1969. He stayed there for seven years. People may wonder how seven years of hard life have shaped his worldview and influenced his policymaking in the present.

Because of the classic capitalism vs. communism debate, Western and Eastern cultures have rarely understood each other, and thus have often been at odds. Therefore, becoming acquainted with this part of history allows the West to comprehend China as an emerging superpower, which is undeniably interwoven into every aspect of the world today: culturally, socially, economically, and literally.

Besides, we should have long gotten past the question, "Will history repeat itself?" and instead remain vigilant in considering, "In what way will history repeat itself?" Extreme ideologies, regardless of the era and system, have a way of dividing people and ripping society apart.

As it turns out, "Heavenly Happiness" has become the first chapter of *From Tea to Coffee*. The comments from my peers' reviews served as a constant source of thrust, prompting me to dig deeper and examine those incidents that caused me to evolve from an idealistic youth to the man I am today.

However, as much as I needed to learn the craft of writing (starting from how to use commas effectively), I equally needed to acquire the ardent spirit to write. I had to step back in time to retrieve the genuine memories of my days and nights from half a century ago. Obviously, I needed to reacquaint myself with those original people and recapture the zeitgeist of 1960s and 1970s China.

As a first step, I went to Daqing Commune to recall my whimsical memories by meeting with my childhood friends. I then traveled back to TianXi to reconnect with the villagers, with whom I once toiled along endless furrows in the cornfields.

Refreshing my mind's eye breathed new life into my old narratives. From cowboy-hood in Daqing at ten (yes, I would ride a cow to herd a dozen others to the fields) to my young adulthood in TianXi, learning the fine art of collecting cow dung for heating and cooking (you must kick the patties first to ensure they are all moistureless—and thus odorless—before picking them up).

Not the least of all, I visited my mom's childhood home, Zhencheng Lou, in a secluded Hakka village nestled deep in the mountain. Her grandfather designed and built this legendary earthen castle 100 years ago. In 2008, Zhencheng Lou and a few others were inscribed by UNESCO as one of the World Cultural Heritage Sites. I wanted to be fully conscious of the strength and courage of the Hakkas that I inherited from my mom. Having a deeper sense of my familial attributes has helped me to understand where my emotions, desires, and audaciousness originated.

Although the places I went to were no longer recognizable today, meeting those I once knew and reminiscing on our past together served to rekindle the intense and complex emotions I held decades ago. It was like lifting the recollection flood gate, causing the people and fateful events from my past to jump into my head uncontrollably, screaming to come out onto the pages.

In addition to my early years in China, I also needed to contemplate my time on the other side of the Pacific. What has edified this 'Educated Youth' after decades of living in America? For one thing, I often wonder why people (even societies) become increasingly obsessed with race and identity. Can't we see each other simply as human beings, each with distinctive traits and personalities? However, before that ideal can be achieved, we must first deal with common ethnic stereotypes.

Asian Americans are characterized—often mythically—as the "model minorities" because of our hard-working, studious, family-oriented, and self-sufficient traditions. But in the meantime, those positive traits have also fueled our own stereotypes: the idea of a people seeking self-preservation by committing no wrong.

One old Chinese saying, "sweep the snow in front of our door, but care nothing about that of others," still holds true today. Unsurprisingly, we are perceived to be one of the most steadfast and unchanging ethnic groups in American society. That includes those of us who have emigrated from China after the 1980s, the exceptionally well-educated, young elites of the country. Our lives are no longer confined to a Chinatown ghetto, yet have we culturally transcended the Chinatown mentality?

"The population of Chinese immigrants in the United States has grown nearly seven-fold since 1980, reaching almost 2.5 million in 2018, or 5.5 percent of the overall foreign-born population." (*Chinese Immigrants in the United States,* Carlos Echeverria-Estrada and Jeanne Batalova, January 15, 2020.) Most of us hold remunerative employment in prestigious companies, but we rarely mix socially outside our familiar communities. While facing anti-Asian incidents, we grumble about 150 years of racism and society ignoring our culture. But perhaps we should also ask ourselves: what have we done to understand their culture?

The latter part of my journey in America ponders these questions: what else can we do collectively to make fundamental changes in others' perceptions of us? It will have to be something more than casting that one vote every four years or congregating and protesting when tragedies occur. We must realize that our flatter cheeks and smaller noses are not at fault, and wearing Anglo first names instead of our native ones will not necessarily make us any less "the other." We can—and we should—take more initiatives to fit in with the larger culture.

Authoring one's first book and being recognized by a well-established publisher is universally acknowledged as one of the most audacious pursuits for a non-native speaker who has never received formal education in English writing. Quite oddly, this entire process, from a random online writing practice to the book hitting the printer, took no more than two years. After innumerable rewritings, developmental evaluation, and editing, I had timidly sent out five query letters. My brief stint joining a local comedy club served me well there: it had not turned me into a comedian, but it had thickened my skin, much-needed protection for a first-time author.

Three weeks later, I miraculously received a couple of replies and then scored a book deal. The rest is history, and you will be the judge of my effort.

This book is not a work of fiction. I believe that real life, as the saying goes, can be stranger and more remarkable than invented tales; therefore, a true story strikes a chord with me more profoundly, despite the fact that no one dies in the end.

This book is also not a history or academic study, and it is not meant to repeat those fully-documented historical events I have referred to, even though I have done plenty of research to ensure that they are correctly recounted. There is no shortage of academic publications that detail all the incidents to be shared among scholars. All too often, however, those writings lack the crucibles of emotion that only the people who have endured those times can truly tell. While readers look to attain intellectual insights through history and academic works, they can expect true emotional experiences through the flesh-and-blood characters in *From Tea to Coffee*.

This memoir recounts the experience of a single Educated Youth: how I went from no secondary education in Mao's era to becoming a Ph.D. candidate at the University of Cincinnati; to go from no formal computer training to becoming the Principal Member of Tech Staff at a major telecom company; and lastly, from having no English writing experience to becoming a published author. As illogical as my life's course may seem, within these pages are the steps I followed each time I reached a crossroad.

Authoring this book has set off another "New Long March" for me, this time detailing the people who crossed paths with me in actual events. In a way, my role in composing this memoir is more like that of a tour guide: revealing history while offering my personal introspection on the events of my lifetime as well as my reactions to landmarks, facts, cultural customs, and, most of all, the people that I encountered along the way. It is, to the best of my memory, a truthful excavation of a life and history that has extended across half a century and across two continents. So I invite you to take this journey with me in the hope that we each emerge more knowledgeable and more tolerant, but most of all, with an appreciation for the struggles, the efforts, and the personal victories of those we might otherwise never have considered.

CHAPTER ONE

"COMMUNISM WILL ONE DAY seize the world," our political economics teacher often lectured as a part of our indoctrination, "and it will happen as naturally as a river flows into the ocean." Growing up in China, this common creed was well-ingrained in us, and at the ripe old age of seventeen, I wanted to play a part in making it happen.

By the time the Great Cultural Revolution had reached its boiling point, I was at the most ambitious stage of my life. Armed with Chairman Mao's thoughts, I was ready to assume my role in emancipating humankind. All the humanities textbooks had instilled in us the idea that human societies evolved in a specific order: primitive, slavery, feudalism, capitalism, socialism, and—guess what came next—communism. Our generation was born precisely to accomplish this mission.

It was a seasonally crisp and sunny day in early September 1975 in Shenyang, my hometown in Northeast China. But, for me, today was anything but normal. I got up much earlier than usual and hurriedly finished my breakfast. I put on a new, pine-green uniform, like those the soldiers wore. Standing in front of a mirror, I strapped a leather belt around my waist and put on a soldier's hat. It made me look and feel resolute. Pinning a red paper flower as big as a frying pan onto my chest—the size and color representing fire and the highest level of enthusiasm—I waved goodbye to my parents. No words were spoken: we did not even make eye contact.

"I will go with you to the train station," my brother offered. He was less than two years older than me, and we had always been close.

"No need for that," I said. Upon second thought, I added, "Or if you want to go, let us meet at the train station." Today I wanted to stand alone, to look like a real soldier, and enjoy this most significant moment in my life.

Marching out to the street, I climbed onto a military truck along with seven others heading to Shenyang Central Railway Station. To me, today was the most celebrated day in the biggest city in Northeastern China. Flowers and colorful streamers hung for miles, announcing the significant event now underway. Red banners strung across intersections displayed the slogans that everyone could recite in those days: *Going to the frontier! Going to the poorest places in China! Going to learn from the peasants!*

The uproar of drums, gongs, and cheering crowds became louder and louder as a single-file procession of military trucks slowly rumbled toward the railway station. Standing on the truck bed, immersed in the great commotion, I felt like a hero in a city of five million people.

For the past nine years, Chairman Mao had orchestrated the Great Cultural Revolution. Now, at the end of middle school, I could not wait to play my part in this unprecedented movement that had swept the entire country. Today, like tens of thousands of Educated Youths before me, I was embarking on a journey to a remote village in Inner-Mongolia, Northern China.

My brother rode his bike to the train station. We then had a photo taken next to the train to record the moment.

There, I met seven other people whose parents also worked under the same Cultural Bureau of Shenyang as my father. Overall, thirty-five of us urban teenagers were destined for the same village in Inner-Mongolia.

"Hey, Wang Cheng!"

I turned to see WuYong, my childhood friend; his father had been a close friend of my parents for many years. He and I were going to the same village. I gave him a brief pat on the shoulder. It was an overwhelming moment for us; after all, we had heard the inspirational tales of all the exemplary urban youths before us. Now, it was my turn. I was imbued with the revolutionary spirit.

With a loud and prolonged whistle, followed by the heavy chuffs from the steam engine, our train pulled out of the station. Settling onto a wooden seat, I removed that enormous paper flower from my chest, as it had already served its purpose. Suddenly, it hit me. For the first time, I had left my comfortable home to go to a place

600 miles away where I had no idea what to expect.

The silence in the train carriage was in sharp contrast to the earlier deafening drumbeats. That, along with constant rhythm of the wheels grinding along the rails, slowed my heartbeat and dimmed my cheeks. Singing from the neighboring carriage lifted my spirits with a prevalent revolutionary song:

"*Let us get together, and tomorrow* The Internationale *shall unite the human race...*"

Apparently, another group of Educated Youths had the same fate as us, but their hearts were still racing faster than the now roaring train.

History had chosen us to break away from our attachments—our families, our friends, our idyllic lives—which we willingly did. But what was to come? That was beyond me. Still, I was unfazed, because I knew I had boarded the right train: our destination was one where everyone would follow, eventually.

CHAPTER TWO

WHILE MY VISION BLURRED within the fast-moving train to TianXi, my mind drifted back to my early childhood, reflecting on how the Cultural Revolution had transformed our family.

We had a comfortable, tender, and caring family back then. I was the youngest, with an older sister and an older brother. I always believed I was the favorite among the three of us. It was a perfect family—if there was such a thing—in the eyes of the surrounding people.

My father started as a playwright. Later, he became the head of the Shenyang Peking Opera Group, the most formal and esteemed opera group in Northeast China. During the Korean War, he once led the Group into North Korea to boost the morale of Chinese soldiers. It made him a well-respected figure at home.

"I was an orphan," my father said to us, more than once. "I started out by cleaning classrooms in schools as a daily duty in exchange for receiving my education—all the way until I finished college." He was enormously proud of his childhood. We knew he had an elder sister who had married at a young age for her survival, because it was impossible for young girls to find decent jobs back then, but there was so much that we did not know. I now wish my father had told us more about his early life.

As much as my father had been a central figure in the Peking Opera Group, our family attracted far more attention because of my mother, one of the very few working women in the Courtyard where we lived whose career had nothing to do with the Peking Opera.

After college, my mother was an editor of a cultural and politically-influential magazine in Shenyang. When the magazine was shut down during the Cultural Revolution, she became a Chinese literature teacher, and then a high school education director.

My mother's early life was very different from my father's. She grew up in an affluent family in Fujian Province, thousands of miles from Shenyang on the southeastern coast of China. Her grandparents were wealthy landlords. Her parents moved to Hong Kong, where her father was an influential newspaper publisher.

My mom graduated from the prestigious Xiamen University in Fujian province, right after the establishment of New China in 1949. She gave up the life already laid out for her—either coming to the U.S. for graduate study or living with her parents in Hong Kong—and instead chose Shenyang. Shenyang was severely in need of people with a college education to help build the city back up after several decades of Japanese occupation followed by civil war. Like so many others at the time, she wholeheartedly embraced the bright prospects of New China.

In comparison, Hong Kong, a British colony back then, was a place flooded with money. People either grew rich then moved to Hong Kong, or became rich after moving there. Many from the Mainland risked their lives by paddling illegally across the sea to Hong Kong. People who knew my mother could not comprehend why she had taken such a different path, one that led her to experience many ups and downs throughout her life.

Nevertheless, my mom's unusual family background provided our family with many rare privileges before the Cultural Revolution. When the country had been decimated by severe famine in the early 1960s (because of The Great Leap Forward economic and social campaign led by Mao from 1958 to 1962), our family received special treatment, such as vouchers for food and other essentials.

Visiting our grandparents was always a joyful time for us all. We would take the train to Guangzhou or Beijing, staying for a week at a time. The government would arrange a luxurious sedan for us with yarn curtains to prevent people from peeking through. We would stay in the best hotel or at an exclusive guesthouse in an enormous, garden-like enclosure: one of the royal residences in the Qing Dynasty. Its gate stayed shut at all times, unless there was a car going in or out. On the outside, people who passed this place every day never knew what it was.

One day in 1965, I recall my mom leaving without telling us where she was going. Later, we found a newspaper on the desk that had her father's obituary. He had apparently died from a heart attack while working at his office desk. In those years, people from the Mainland were not allowed to go to Hong Kong unless it was for an unusual—and often undisclosed—reason. Premier Zhou Enlai sent his personal condolences to my mother's family, a tremendous honor and acknowledgment for my grandfather's achievements.

When Mao launched the Cultural Revolution in May 1966, he aimed to curb rising bourgeois values, resuscitate the revolutionary spirit, and strengthen his supremacy in the CCP (Chinese Communist Party). His grassroots method was to incite ordinary workers and students to challenge all authority except himself. Mao enthused fervent students to organize themselves as "Red Guards" to target the establishment, the "Old Guards," and intellectuals, including people with complicated family histories—all those most likely to have inclinations toward capitalism and revisionism.

Subsequently, "the workers, peasants, and soldiers" became the central revolutionary force. They ascended to the top of the social hierarchy, taking over leadership positions in all organizations, including research and academic institutes, and they purged the people in the leadership positions.

Amidst the high-pressure politics of those years, no one attempted to make sense of what was happening. In the same way, few ever questioned why scholars and intellectuals had suddenly descended to the lowest echelons of society. The once-lofty status of those who possessed a college education (or higher) had fallen below the other eight classes: landlord, rich peasant, counter-revolutionary, outlaw, rightist, spy, traitor, and capitalist. Thus, intellectuals during the Cultural Revolution were nicknamed the 'Stinking Ninths,' a term that evolved from one radically popular belief at the time: the more knowledge you had, the more reactionary you would become.

My parents both had graduated from college shortly after the founding of New China, which was uncommon and rightfully respected at the time. But ironically, during the years of the Cultural Revolution, they found that they were the ones on the wrong side of the tracks.

CHAPTER THREE

IN MY CHILDHOOD MEMORY, it was when I was around seven that both my parents suddenly turned out to be 'Stinking Ninths.' As if overnight, a caring and loving family became distant with few words to say to one another. It was the first time our family was caught in the political undertow, and it threatened to pull us all under.

My father, the head of the Peking Opera Group, was sidelined. They picked a stage janitor to assume his role. The janitor's family lived in the same building we lived in. The place was a huge, four-story, L-shaped building. All the families living there had one or both parents working in the Shenyang Peking Opera Group as actors, musicians, stage workers, and electricians.

In that building, everyone knew everyone. As a result, this place earned a nickname known to those even living many blocks away: the Peking Opera Courtyard. There were about 100 families living in this walled compound with an enormous courtyard at the center and only one main entry, making it an exceptionally safe and cozy place for the kids to play (not as big as I remembered, however, when I went back to visit it many years later. Somehow, everything became smaller!).

The custodian-turned-group-leader transformed himself overnight by taking off his greasy, blue overalls and putting on a brand-new soldier's uniform sporting a red armband with "Rebel" imprinted on it. His son, who was around eight, a similar age to me, loved scavenging in one of the big dumpsters in the Courtyard and was thus nicknamed Lajisho (garbage hand). One day, Lajisho suddenly told us which games we could play and who could play them—and who could not.

"You, the bourgeoisie's cub, out!" Lajisho pointed at me.

I could not figure out why, and I felt deeply hurt. In tears, I ran home to my father. "Why did Lajisho keep me out of the game?" I whined to him.

"You two do not belong to the same frontline anymore," my father responded, more amused than I was, and as though he had seen it coming. "But I will play with you."

Like a gigantic vortex, this political movement caught every family in the country and pulled them down with it. For me, life was not too bad in the beginning. While they removed my father from work (without stopping his monthly salary), he spent the daytime practicing calligraphy, Tai Chi, and playing chess with my brother or me. He often remarked that I was the better player, which only made me want to play more.

At home, I noticed a few changes, such as a much bigger fish tank and more plants. By that summer, my father would let me sit on the back of his bike while he pedaled to a river outside the city to swim. I would float in the water, facing down with my father's enormous hand under my belly, both my arms paddling as he instructed me.

"You do breaststrokes when you want to swim a longer distance," my father said while he showed me with his other arm in the water, "and you do the crawl for speed."

On our way home he would buy me popsicles and other various nibbles that I craved. Those days have stayed with me my entire life. They were instrumental in starting my first hobby—swimming— which has never worn off. I still do breaststrokes and a crawl interchangeably when I swim, and I often feel like my father is near me.

During that time, my mom was still working at her high school as the education director. There was a giant dumpster outside of her office window, and I would climb on top of it and open the window to let myself in when she was not there. I looked for snacks or wrote things on the blackboard, pretending to be a teacher: the most admirable figure, in my mind. Many teachers and students in that building knew me and loved to tease me, which made my mom's school a fun place for me to go.

However, one day, my mom told me not to come to the school anymore, and she began to arrive home much later than usual. One evening, I was at home by myself. It was already dark outside. My mom came home and lumbered past me without a word. I felt like I was in a daze watching her, as she did not even turn on the lights. She simply lay down on her bed. I went to her and quietly lay down beside her. It was then that I felt dried, hardened paste with pieces of newspaper glued all over to her clothes. I could only guess what had happened as she held me closer to her in silence. Tears streamed down my face and into my ear, as I lay sideways in the darkness. That night I cried myself to sleep.

It was a common scene in those days. We often saw Red Guards place one or two people on the stage, wearing three-foot-tall, pointed paper hats. The people onstage had to bend their backs at a forty-five-degree angle to beg for leniency. Papers with shaming words were glued to their clothes, and cardboard hung around their necks by a string. On the cardboard was written things like "Anti-Revolutionist," "Traitor," or "Spy." Sometimes two bricks were added to the line around their neck to force the person to bend even lower to break both their physical and mental strength. Dozens of the Red Guards would surround the stage, shouting slogans; some spat and threw trash onto the stage. Eventually, the person in the center would confess something about their antirevolutionary past just to end the humiliation. I pictured my mom standing on that stage, surrounded by all the fanatical Red Guards. The scene forever burned one of the most insulting, abusive, and painful images in my memory.

A few days later, several Red Guards kicked our door open and came in to turn all the drawers and suitcases upside down. They took away many photos of my mom with her parents which were taken in Hong Kong, her two brothers, and her sister as the evidence. My mom's younger sister and her husband, a naval officer of the Republic of China, followed the former President Chiang Kai-shek to Taiwan, where he retreated after losing the civil war to Mao. My mom's elder brother was once a high-ranking navy officer under Chiang, whose family moved to the U.S. Those were the worst nightmares for families in those days.

Many people committed suicide during the Cultural Revolution because they could not take the abuse—the Red Guards' insults and torture went on day and night. Worst of all, their children joined the Red Guards, aligning against their parents, to prove their worldview was entirely in line with the revolutionists. Through all of this, my mom kept her feelings, opinions, and even her fears inside. This I could barely imagine, even decades later.

Indeed, the Red Guards singled out my mother because of her complicated family relationship at the start of the Cultural Revolution. Not that my mother thought there was something wrong with herself or her family, but it was impossible to reason with the young, reckless Red Guards, who were insanely committed and utterly senseless in those years. However, knowing myself as being quixotic in nature, I cannot say that I would have been more rational if I had been old enough to join them. Thanks to the fateful age disparity in those years, I was too young for that elite Red Guard title, which was for high-schoolers or college-age kids.

My father, on the other hand, was "politically pure" in the words of those years. And yet, he had married someone who came from a wealthy and now suspicious family, a mistake that planted an ominous seed in their relationship for the rest of their lives.

My father grumbled to me once that he could have been appointed to a much higher official position if not for my mom's family background. For the same reason, my mom also mentioned to me—unregretfully though—that she could have been the high school principal long ago had her family's background not failed her politically.

After the Red Guards investigated my mom, there was little laughter and hardly any words of affection exchanged within the family. For all the teenage children, myself included, we needed to pick a side—the right side, if we wanted to have any future. The three of us—my elder sister, my brother, and I—never talked about how our parents' circumstances would affect our futures. My brother and my sister did not seem bothered by the circumstances. In fact, they both had their own calculations. Because of their distinctive talents—my sister became a performing artist and my brother was admitted into the Shenyang Conservatory of Music at a young age—they both managed to stay out of politics during those years.

As one of the Educated Youths (the official label for those of us from middle school to college age), I felt the need to stay far away from the 'Stinking Ninths' in order to maintain the appearance of supporting Chairman Mao's leadership. I knew I must answer the call of a lifetime by going to the most rural, impoverished area for re-education. "On my mission to break the chains of the working-class people in the world, I first have to break my chains to my family," I vowed in my head.

For me, by nature or by fate, I was on the path to becoming a Maoist soldier. My destiny was TianXi. I was inspired by the "Long March" led by Mao in 1934. That famous military retreat lasted twenty-four months and covered six thousand miles. It enabled the survival of his Red Army, allowing them to break through Nationalist enemy lines and establish Yan'an as the birthplace of the revolution.

I knew I could do it, physically. Mentally, I prepared for my New Long March by reading the novel, *How the Steel Was Tempered*, for the third time. It was a socialistic novel written by Nikolai Ostrovsky in the 1930s Soviet Union era. From this book, I wrote down the most popular quote at the time in my diary:

> *"Man's dearest possession is life. It is given to him but once, and he must live it so as to feel no torturing regrets for wasted years, never know the burning shame of a mean and petty past; so live that, dying, he might say: all my life, all my strength were given to the finest cause in all the world—the fight for the Liberation of Mankind."*—Nikolai Ostrovsky

It fueled my passion and made me think about how the protagonist of the novel, Pavel Korchagin, survived his revolutionary experience while fighting for Soviet Bolsheviks. Mostly, I pictured how I could be like him—to be transformed from a mischievous boy into an idealistic, revolutionary soldier. I wanted to be as strong as steel and become like Pavel.

But that book branded my coming-of-age in a peculiar way during a very peculiar time.

Chapter Four

After three grueling days of travel—the first two on a train, the third on a bus and, for the last five miles, a horse-drawn cart—the drum-beating crowd became a distant memory. So did the ecstasy on my face. Four deep tracks on the muddy road, two in each direction, spoke of the constant grinding of horse-drawn carts, which was the most lavish means of transportation within a ten-mile radius, above donkey carts and your own feet.

What finally came into view were a few dozen houses erected on both sides of a curvy, marshy road—the only 'thoroughfare' leading to the village. These were the locals' dwellings. They were all rectangular in shape, built entirely with mud and thatched with straw. A thin, white paper was the material of choice to cover front windows instead of glass.

Fall came as early as September in Northern China. Naked trees under the low-hanging clouds dotted the bare land around the yellowish houses. All the walls and houses were built using the soil from the ground on which they stood, thus painting a broad landscape of the same muddy color as far as my eyes could see. A corresponding earthy odor scented the air.

The frigid fall, plus the chilly ambiance, seeped through my soldier-like uniform, causing me to shiver. Some peasants came out to look on curiously, as if aliens had made an uninvited landing and entered their settlement. Chickens and ducks ran around leisurely, contributing a trivial, yet much needed liveliness to the backdrop.

Finally, the three pure Mongolian horses pulled our cart into a courtyard surrounded by mud walls and a wood-log gate, which served as the village center. The village's unassuming office was no better than its residences except for its much larger size and an eye-catching plaque that hung above a handmade, two-panel door, reading: TianXi (which means "Heavenly Happiness" in direct translation). That was the name of this village, with its population of 250 people.

TianXi was a production team under the jurisdiction of the TianShan People's Commune. Before the early 1980s, the People's Commune was the de facto collective system in all the rural areas, one of many social and economic structures that Mao had replicated from 'Big Brother:' the Soviet Union.

Long before coming here, I had conceived a mental picture of Inner Mongolia from Chinese literature and poems: of rolling hills with bright green meadows reaching for the clear blue sky, and, as one Chinese poet famously put it, "Under the sky and on earth, breeze lowers flora to reveal flocks and herds." And yet, in front of me was a scene for which I was entirely unprepared. Furthermore, the social aspect differed dramatically from pictures I had seen in the media. Where were the fireworks and flags? Shouldn't there be villagers on both sides of the road holding out their homegrown fruits or, at least, water? Where were the decorative dormitories, ready for us to move in? When ideals met my reality, the former disappeared as rapidly as a mouse sighting a cat, and the initial chill that had gripped this unworldly, seventeen-year-old city boy grew.

Was this where I would spend my youthful years—possibly the rest of my life—to receive my re-education and carry the revolutionary torch forward to become an ever-purer proletariat? Of course, if this was the highest calling any person could achieve, how could it be wrong? My inner voice served to suppress any encroaching doubts even before they could surface. I, like millions of others all over China, honestly believed in this course, the one that would lead to a better world for humankind.

Therefore, during those years, when even the slightest doubt felt like the opposite of faith, self-recrimination had become a daily ritual to eradicate any reservations before they could properly emerge. If others could do it, I whispered silently, so could I!

In fact, based on records there were already sixteen million Educated Youths who had been sent on the same path now before me during the previous eight years of the Cultural Revolution, including some from the most notable families in the country.

Deng Xiaoping's three children were among them (Deng later reformed the economy in the early 1980s and opened China to the Western world). His second daughter, Deng Nan, was dispatched from Beijing University to a village in Shanxi Province. His youngest daughter, Deng Rong, and his youngest son, Deng Zhifang, had been sent to the countryside for re-education several years earlier. Most of all, Xi Jinping himself (Xi has served as General Secretary of the Chinese Communist Party and Chairman of the Central Military Commission from 2012 to the present day) was an Educated Youth. He was sent to Liangjiahe Village on the Loess Plateau, one of the most impoverished regions in Northwestern China, in 1969 at age fifteen. He remained there for seven years. And here I was, in my own choice of a rural location in Inner Mongolia. My new life in TianXi had begun.

While I was in a daze with myriad impressions and unanswered questions crowding my thoughts, a middle-aged man with tanned skin, broad shoulders, and a genial smile strode out of the village office's double doors. His Mao-style suit had a few patches on the elbows and shoulders but was otherwise neat and clean. "Welcome to TianXi!" he said while his bright eyes swept across our young, pale faces. His two sturdy arms reached out to shake hands with those of us in the front. Another man, who came out after him, introduced the middle-aged man as the TianXi Production Team's party secretary. His surname was Cong, so we all referred to him as Secretary Cong.

That introduction broke the silence amongst us thirty-six newcomers and spread weary smiles across our worry-filled faces. We then followed our party secretary into his office. Inside, on one side of the room, were two wooden benches situated around a handmade table. The other side of the room, by the front windows, was a wall-to-wall 'warm bed' or *huokang*, which was common in rural regions of Northern China. But to most city dwellers like ourselves, huokang was fascinating, partly because of its size—it took up almost half the room—but more so because it was warm in its entirety. We all rushed to get onto it, to feel the warmth it filled the room with, and to seek out how it worked.

"The first lesson for your re-education is huokang," Secretary Cong said casually, seeing us drawn to this common local fixture.

"Huokang were started many hundreds of years ago by Manchus. They lived in the northeast region, where winter was exceedingly long and frigid. So, they designed this cost-effective heating method, which has lasted until now because winter is still long and cold." His easygoing speech evoked cheery chuckles about the room. He then pointed to the huokang, like a science teacher giving a lecture. The bed's surface was a number of stone slabs sealed by mud and supported by mud-bricks from below. From the kitchen in the adjacent room, the stove would send the heat from one end of the huokang, pass it underneath the entire bed, and then out the other end, which was connected to the chimney on the outer wall. Cooking became the only source of heat for the huokang, and through it, the entire room, all day long. It was—and still is in most areas—one of the most intelligent designs to both cook and warm a room during six bleak winter months in Northern China.

We then saw a gigantic, cast-iron wok about four feet in diameter set in a cornstalk-burning stove in the kitchen. Our eyes followed Secretary Cong's hand gestures in a way we never had in any of our previous classes.

As Secretary Cong continued, his radiant eyes cast his direct gaze over us, and his firm tone had a distinctive effect upon me. In fact, he seemed to care about us, perhaps eager for the opportunity to mold these urban teens into more robust human beings. In his eyes, we were all spoiled, city boys who had never touched a shovel. And he was mostly right.

"We are currently building dorms for all of you, one for boys and one for girls," he announced. "However, until the project has been completed, you will each live with a designated host family."

What would my hosts be like? And what would they think of me?

CHAPTER FIVE

FOUR OF US WERE assigned to a host family, a modest-looking couple in their late forties with a son and a daughter who were two and three years younger than us. However, their timid eyes made them look far younger than that.

We walked to our temporary home, a typical straw-thatched mud house that was divided into three sections. In such dwellings, the middle area of the house, where the primary entrance was located, contained the kitchen. On both sides of the kitchen, there were two familiar woks just like the one we saw in the village center a moment ago. The woks setting in the similar stoves connected the huokangs in the two adjacent rooms on each side—obviously one room for the host family and another they had prepared for the newcomers. Our host family's surname was Liu, so we all called the man Uncle Liu and his wife Aunt Liu. We followed Uncle Liu into the kitchen area and he pointed to the left side of the room and gestured for us to enter without a word. Inside our room, I saw the wall-to-wall huokang by the front windows, just like what Secretary Cong told us that every household had in the same way. It took up half of the room, which was more than enough space for the four of us. I saw no furniture inside; therefore, this huokang would serve as chair, table, and stand for doing anything during the day—and a bed for the four of us at night. Yellowish newspapers covered the interior walls and ceiling, and the scent of smoldering cornstalks permeated the air. During the day, soft sunlight poured in through the thin, white paper pasted over the wood-framed windows, radiating warmth all over and relaxing my mind.

We put down our luggage on the huokang with enormous sighs of relief. Our hosts' two children peeked out at us each time we

16

passed through the kitchen area as if we had come from Mars. The family was noticeably quiet, only uttering a few words at a time meant only to be audible between them. However, the old couple's heavily tanned, wrinkled but affable faces and uneven yellow teeth, so much resembling deflated corn kernels, all indicative of their humble and unassuming demeanor, made me feel at ease.

Just when we wanted to sit down and take a breather from our long journey, Uncle Liu appeared at the door. "Time to eat," he said.

We flocked to the wok in the kitchen while Uncle Liu lifted the lid, allowing steam to escape and revealing ten golden pieces of cornbread stuck to the side of the wok. On the bottom of the wok simmered potato and cabbage stew, releasing a mouth-watering aroma into the air. Egg flowers floated in the stew, a most luxurious food item that the villagers would only use for a special occasion.

"If still hungry, come again for more." Aunt Liu saw us hesitate and sensed correctly that we were considering how much to take.

They had made the cornbread by mixing the freshest corn with water, and its moist but firm texture, plus its natural syrupiness, was unlike any cornmeal I had ever eaten. This meal certainly seemed better than anything we'd had in the city, but perhaps that was because it was the only hot meal we'd had after three days and nights of cold food during travel.

For the moment, I put everything—my family, my 600-mile distant home, my paranoia, and even the dim prospect of my future—behind me. Starting today, this would be my home.

That evening, Secretary Cong organized a welcome gathering for the newcomers. The villagers had never seen so many young and pale faces, not to mention the various colors and styles of dress. However, I couldn't go because one of our roommates, Xiao Wei, the youngest in our group, had buried his face beneath his pillow, and was weeping. "I have a toothache," he murmured in his trembling voice from underneath the pillow. "I miss my home."

I was the eldest by two years, and somehow I felt responsible for him. So I stayed. I wasn't sure what to say, because the thought "I miss home" had not yet appeared in my head. We had only just arrived, after all, and it was only the beginning of what would be a presumably long stay.

Suddenly, I realized this may be precisely the reason they should send young people like us to this far-flung corner of the world: we would all miss our homes from time to time, but we couldn't just go home when we wanted to. We really had no choice but to stay and receive re-education. But I couldn't say that to Xiao Wei just then—I had to try to encourage him.

"There is a party to attend," I said, "and everyone is there now." I paused, trying to find the right words. "You know, we should be there now to meet the peasants, like everyone else."

As I was trying to further reassure Xiao Wei, Aunt Liu showed up at the door. In her hands she held a bowl with steam rising from it. One of the most comforting delights, it was a bowl of steamed egg custard. Just beat two eggs in a bowl, adding twice as much water and a bit of salt, sesame oil, and chopped green onion. Steam for five to seven minutes until the egg and water are firm, and it is ready to serve.

She had made it for Xiao Wei when she'd heard his weeping chatter. (It was and still is the best and most soothing cure for people who cannot chew—even more so for those who are homesick at the same time.)

Aunt Liu put the bowl down on the huokang in front of Xiao Wei and turned without a word, all before Xiao Wei could even say thank you. Xiao Wei finished eating, wiped the tears from his eyes, and then agreed to go to the party with me.

Following the party noise, Xiao Wei and I made it to the crowd. In the open space outside the Production Team Office, everyone sat on the wooden benches in a large half-circle. I picked a seat beside a man Secretary Cong introduced as Director Tao, the second-in-command after Secretary Cong. He was in his forties. When he greeted me with a warm smile, his round, tanned face wrinkled. His softer tone of voice—in contrast with the assertiveness of Secretary Cong—and his approachable demeanor made me comfortable sitting by his side.

"I was born, grew up, and have spent all my life here in TianXi," Director Tao said to me. He had followed Chairman Mao when he'd led the villagers against their landlords during the civil war. After the founding of New China, the People's Commune had seized ownership of the land; hence, all the peasants became landowners, and everyone was now equal within society.

Most people in this village had never been anywhere else, and life here had always been challenging. The farmland was too dry, along with a short growing season in Northern China, making agricultural life difficult. But Director Tao believed that Chairman Mao would again lead them to overcome the harsh conditions and somehow become prosperous. Apparently, the poorest were the most loyal followers of Mao. So it made sense for Mao to send us here to learn from these peasants and become as loyal to the revolution as they were.

Decades later, when I returned to TianXi and visited Director Tao's home, he and his wife were not much better off than poor church mice. Yet, on the wall, in the most central location directly above the huokang, I saw two large, framed portraits: one of Mao and one of Xi, ritually side by side. They would be the allies to revolutionize the world—if that could ever happen.

I pondered: How could these peasants, who could barely produce enough to sustain themselves, possibly be able to liberate the world?

A local girl interrupted my train of thought. Approaching me, she held a bowl of hot tea in her hands. Her eyes were lowered; she said not one word, even when I thanked her. Milk tea, as they called it, was one of the most prevalent delights throughout Mongolia.

Director Tao saw me pause. "Try it," he said. "This is one of the simplest, but one of the best delicacies that we can offer our guests."

My first few sips were tentative; it tasted unlike anything I had ever tried before. I learned from Director Tao that it was made of fermented tea and boiled in a mix of water and horse milk (cow milk would do as well), and then stir-fried millet and salt added to it. "Very good!" I said to Director Tao with a satisfied smile on my face.

While I savored the tea, I watched the city girls sing in front of the crowd while a few of the locals performed typical Mongolian dances. My attention was drawn to the people of both worlds, locals and the urban newcomers. The girls still giggled in the same beguiling way when gazing at goofy boys. And boys still laughed at inane teenage jokes. But there were obvious distinctions between the two worlds that were now merged by edict and highlighting one bizarreness of the situation thanks to the Cultural Revolution.

Still, the same uneasiness seemed to linger in the minds of everyone at the moment: living together, working side-by-side in the fields with our backs to the sky and faces to the earth, how long could we youths, "sent-down" from the cities, last? The peasants suspected us—as much as we questioned ourselves. Could we endure this naturally harsh landscape and difficult lifestyle? And if so, for how long?

CHAPTER SIX

THE NEXT DAY, I followed my inquisitive instinct to stroll around and check out this rustic, medieval-like settlement. Why was this place chosen for our re-education?

Mud-and-straw-thatched houses lined each side of the road and radiated out into alleyways on the hill. All the front windows faced south, to make them energy efficient. Every house had a square front yard that served as an open space for chickens, ducks, and pigs to forage, and a small backyard to grow vegetables and tobacco. However, there were no swings or climbing bars for the kids. Children do not play here, I speculated. They begin to help with the work from the day they can walk.

The environment was grim, secluded, and, most of all, monotonous. My thoughts raced as I wandered through the village. Had they ever seen or even heard of such places as movie theaters, post offices, banks, temples, or churches? A bakery or barbershop? Apparently, they had no need for any of these, I surmised.

From Director Tao I learned a few rudimentary truths in TianXi. Eggs served as the currency for the locals. They used eggs to exchange for everyday essentials such as salt, cloth, farm tools, and notebooks for school children. One had to drive a donkey cart for half a day to bring a basket of eggs to barter for necessities in the Cooperative Supply Store near the Commune Center.

People worked for an entire year to get their rationed grains from the Production Unit. The number of people in their household and the weather conditions for that year would determine how much they received. However, the food crops that they received were always two or three months short, even in a decent year, before the earth could turn those sprouts into edible yields. People needed to be creative, usually by adding more sweet potato or tree leaves to mix with grains in order to get by. Life here functioned around sunrise and sunset. No one ever needed a watch. Entertainment? What entertainment?

But what occupied their minds? I wondered. What made them feel alive in this solitary and indifferent corner of the world? As I considered my own questions, a ten-foot-long red banner on the mud wall caught my eye. The large text in bold, black font read: "Carrying out the Great Proletarian Cultural Revolution to the End." Those were Mao's words in 1966, when he initiated that unprecedented movement. It jolted me back to reality.

The same faithful spirit that took control of the minds of everyone, including the people in this lonesome outpost, left no room for second guessing. Thus, one color, one style of dwelling, one pace in life, and one idea for every mind; all of which made TianXi the perfect place for us to receive our re-education, to reinforce this one solitary ideology in all of us.

Secretary Cong allowed us a few days to adjust to the new living conditions. But soon our honeymoon period was over, and all thirty-six of us urban teens were now expected to do the same farming work as the locals. That was the reason we had come here.

There were two Production Units under the TianXi Production Team—Unit One and Unit Two—which divided the households in the village into two parts for labor management and accounting purposes. They divided the thirty-six of us evenly into both Production Units, and I was assigned to Unit Two.

Late September was the busiest and most exhilarating time of year—harvest time. TianXi was deep in Inner-Mongolia, where a nomadic lifestyle was once the tradition, not agriculture. Over the years, the pasture available for grazing had shrunk, more Han people moved in, and permanent houses replaced the gers (also known as yurts, the portable, round tent covered with sheep skins or felt that was used as a dwelling by nomadic tribes). Now, like most other agricultural areas in Northeastern China, TianXi grew mostly corn, soybeans, and sorghum as the staple.

The villagers couldn't wait for us to join them in bringing in the crops, and I couldn't wait to try my hands at it. Most educated youths did not feel that way, although it was not as if they had any choice in the matter. Each of us had received a brand-new sickle from our Production Unit. I spent two hours sharpening my sickle the night before to make sure it was ready to go.

Working on my sickle and visualizing the now familiar, open-crop field, I was whisked back to the three years of my childhood in Daqing Commune when my parents took Chairman Mao's "5.7 Road."

In 1968, our parents took the "5.7 Road," a movement named after Mao's prominent announcement on May 7, 1966. Mao had suggested that the entire countryside act as one large school, and urged intellectuals to go to the vast agricultural "classroom" for spiritual cleansing. Naturally, both of my parents were on that list, and actually, it turned out to be a relief for us, especially for my mom, because she was able to avoid the abusive, volatile Red Guards, and possibly diverting the unimaginable from happening.

Following Mao's "5.7 Road" order, our family of five loaded all our belongings onto a military truck. We then settled in Daqing Commune in TiaLing County, forty kilometers from Shenyang. We lived in Daqing Commune for three years before the government arranged for my parents to move back to Shenyang, about the time that I started middle school. During those three years in Daqing, I was too young to care about the brutal politics. In fact, those years were filled with magical memories of my childhood.

At ten, I was intrigued by my environment. I was able to easily make friends, and I relished an unconstrained life in the vast open countryside. We still had to go to school, but we seldom sat in the classroom. There was always a need for help in the fields, which we willingly did in the spirit of learning from the peasants.

My mom often packed more cookies for me than I could eat each day, and I would share them with my friends. Most rural kids had never touched store-bought cookies, which later became one of the more memorable aspects about me when we all met again several decades later.

During the Daqing's farming seasons, as little kids we usually followed a plow pulled by two horses—or trailed its wafting earthy scent—to sow seeds in the freshly-opened soil. The musky odor was irresistible to me.

Weeks later, we would come back with hoes to weed and loosen the soil around the seedlings. Then the fields were plowed again using the horses. This practice was repeated three times before fruition, when we joined the harvesting forces. As kids, we often worked half a day—just enough for fun—before returning to the school playground or wherever else my curiosity led me.

No one seemed to mind that school-age children spent most of their time away from classrooms—my parents never did, and neither did I. Therefore, I was a free spirit, with plenty of time to wander and explore.

My elder sister and brother were also in Daqing, but never showed the slightest curiosity in the rural parish. The far-and-wide, smelly, dusty terrain seemed to turn them off. They often found some excuses to stay at home instead of going to the farm fields.

Somehow, as a kid growing up in the city, I was fascinated by the rolling hills, the green meadows, and the horse-drawn wagons on the dusty throughway. The clippity-clop of hooves striking the ground always made me pause, drawing my eyes to follow the carriage. Watching the blacksmith nail horseshoes onto the horses' hooves was fascinating to me. I would often forget how late it was before heading home. Then again, what was the rush? It was not as if I had school assignments to finish.

But, by far, the most carefree merriment I experienced in Daqing was when I got to work as a cowherd one summer. Another local boy had been tasked by the Commune to herd a dozen cows to the field during the day for grazing, and then bring them back in the evening. At thirteen, he was a few years older than I was. But possibly because of his slim body and tiny size, he was seen as a nonentity in everyone's eyes, and no one ever used his actual name. Instead, they just called him Xiao Ren ('a little person').

Each morning Xiao Ren would drive the cows out of the village, and when he was near my home, he would blow a whistle. I would grab whatever food I could find from the kitchen and rush out to join him. I always went for the golden cow, who had come to know me quite well after our first few encounters. She slowed down when I approached her, then stood still, waving her big tail to greet me. I patted her neck and led her to a big rock on the roadside. I stepped on the rock to climb onto her bare, bony back.

"You ride a cow close to the front legs, and a donkey close to its back legs, but you ride a horse in the middle," Xiao Ren taught me. We drove the rest of the cows for forty minutes through the village to a small meadow by the river. We would then leave them there for the day and come back for them before dark. As I watched Xiao Ren, short and slender as he was and rarely saying a word, yet confident in handling many cows all by himself, I felt a bit of envy. In my eyes, he had the best job in the world, though he had never spent a single day in school.

Now in TianXi, I was to be a full-grown workhand myself, and I could not wait to answer the highest calling from Chairman Mao.

Every household had a broadcast speaker hanging above the bedroom door, a small wooden box that was wired directly to the Production Unit Center. Before daybreak during the busy season, each Production Unit Captain would broadcast to their entire labor force—as young as twelve to as old as seventy—where to go and what to do for that day. That way, everyone knew what tool to bring with them and could go directly to their designated field. We—all the Educated Youths, young and energetic as we were—belonged to the main production force, which was comprised of the strongest men and women.

While it was still dark outside, the four of us in our host family rose at the first call from the speaker. Aunt Liu had a basket of warm cornbread out by the wok, garnished with a plate of salted radish, a typical side dish year-round. I put on a heavy jacket and tightened a leather belt over my jacket for the chilly morning. My sickle was underneath my arm, with a piece of salted radish in one hand and cornbread in the other as the four of us dragged our rigid, drowsy bodies toward the Production Unit.

The eastern horizon glowed soft red. Rejuvenating moisture emanated from the morning dew, adding to the ambiance and reaching the deepest part of my lungs. Several roosters crowed to awaken the universe. White smoke curled from chimneys, suggesting that the village was awakening. Nature and humans resonated in harmony, blending the seemingly disparate elements into a state of serenity I had never experienced in the city. This, perhaps, was the reason people had settled here; it was a place they felt grounded, a place they rightfully belonged to, from generation to generation.

I wondered, how did I fit in here? And what might I learn? Would I be like a cloud, randomly passing by, or a tree putting down roots?

CHAPTER SEVEN

WE FOLLOWED OUR PRODUCTION Unit Captain on a curvy, muddy road which had been deeply furrowed over the years by passing horse-drawn carts. Thirty minutes later, we stopped at one end of a cornfield. In front of us lay an ocean of yellow corn stalks. And we were here to cut them down with our sickles, one by one, and tie them up and haul them away. My childhood idol, Pavel Korchagin from the novel *How the Steel Was Tempered*, entered my thoughts to firm my resolve—I knew I could do it!

"Each one takes a furrow," the captain ordered. "Do not pass the Lead. Start!" There was always a lead person to control the quality and pace for each group of people working on the farm field.

I plunged into the ocean of cornstalks. Bending my back, extending the sickle forward as far as I could, I then pulled back the sharpened tool to cut the lowest part of five or six tall stalks. My left arm opened to catch them. I repeated this two or three times until my underarm held enough stalks. Setting them down on the field, I used a stem to tie the rest in a knot. Once tied, the rolls of stalks were left on the field to be collected and thrown onto a horse cart. I kept my head down, eyes on the tip of my sweeping sickle, and chugged along.

After a while, I noticed the sun was much higher and the temperature was warmer (here time was not defined by hours) and I found myself surrounded by only the rustling corn leaves. There was no end in sight to the cornfield. My teenage body was strong, and my fluid motion worked like a well-oiled machine. Occasionally, I stood up and stretched my back. I took a few deep breaths as I surveyed my work and was overjoyed at the sight of several dozen rolls of stalks lying on the ground behind me. Then I spotted one row of stalks that stood alone, and I noticed that it was my roommate Xiao Wei who was slogging through it. A few of the locals were relaxing nearby since they were so far ahead of us newcomers. Some seemed to take pleasure in watching 'educated' city youths learn how to do simple farm labor. Two comments reached my ears: "City food is not for raising strong bodies," said one worker. "And textbooks don't help much either," said another. They laughed knowingly.

Seeing Xiao Wei and a few others left so far behind, coupled with hearing those comments, was a little hurtful. I walked over and started cutting toward Xiao Wei along his furrow. Then another city girl, who was also fast, came over to lend her hands, and then another. Soon a friendly rivalry developed between the newcomers and the locals. Before long, the mocking comments disappeared, and then some locals came to help the few newcomers that had been left behind. In their eyes we city youngsters must have looked awkward in the field; but when they realized how hard we tried, their compassion took over.

Finally, we all neared the end of our furrows. Seeing all the pink, sweaty faces of the urban youths glowing under the sun, I was certain that was how I looked. Deep inside I found the physical exertion exhilarating, which stemmed from a mixed feeling of assimilating, contending, and, most of all, our emotional state shifting. A young, local man named Ma Lin was working at my side. He gestured for me to rest. He was around my age, six feet tall with pleasant-looking eyes on a well-proportioned face. He was one of very few in TianXi who had completed middle school. He handed me a pouch of loose tobacco and a piece of white paper for rolling a cigarette. I saw how he did it, but that piece of paper seemed unmanageable in my hand. Without a word, he quickly wrapped another and handed it to me, lighting a match when he was done.

As soon as I drew in a slight puff, the pungent and bitter odor burned my tongue and stuck in my throat. The locals called it HaMaLia ("toad" in translation) because of the coarse appearance of its dried leaves and, most of all, its intensity. I was all tears and coughed uncontrollably.

"You will get used to it," Ma Lin said, as if he had expected what this tobacco would do to me. He then picked up my sickle and pulled out a small sharpening stone from his pocket, grinding it along the blade a few times. "It's sharp, but the handle is new; it will blister your hand before your hand grows accustomed to it," Ma Lin said to me, a genial smile on his face. "But you did alright."

"Our family lived in the countryside for a few years when I was little, so it's not wholly new to me." I looked at his sickle; the blade was sharp and much narrower because of its constant use, and the handle was smooth and shiny. But his palm was dull and rough, like tree bark. I then looked at my right palm, its tender, ivory tone now turning pink and feeling fiery. This, I told myself, was but one lesson in "learning from the peasants." With my gaze fixed upon the sickle, the reiteration of its symbolic meaning reassured me.

Chinese textbooks taught us that the sickle is an exceptional icon; together with a hammer on the backdrop of a red field, it is the emblem of the Communist Party of China. It signifies the union of the working classes, which was first adopted by the Soviets during the Russian Revolution. Now, with a sickle in my hand, I felt that destiny was unmistakably on my side.

CHAPTER EIGHT

EVERY MONTH I WOULD receive a package from my mom, which often included a *People's Literature* magazine and a letter, plus some cash. She always knew what I needed. The message was brief, though, unlike many heartbroken, deeply concerned mothers who often wrote to their children in tears, picturing the hardship their children must be enduring. My mom never seemed to worry about me facing a hard life. Instead, she would often encourage me to be respectful in the grand social classroom, "to be humble and to learn from the poor and low-middle peasants," in Mao's words.

Absence makes the heart grow fonder. I understood this saying only when I was by myself, 600 miles away from the people who loved me. My mom's letters often triggered my memories of a picture-perfect, most endearing family before this political upheaval. However, what used to be the worthy elements of a family—high education, privileged parents, well-heeled siblings, and relatives in the Western countries—had suddenly turned against us.

My mom, having all those on her record, was labeled as an enemy of the state in the eyes of Red Guards. But she never held a grudge against anyone, and never shed tears in front of us. The thought of this—although I could never understand it fully—strengthened my resolve to overcome the hardship I now faced.

The series of political rifts from the 1950s to the early 1970s had turned people against one other, including friends and family members. When people come to China today, they often sense this lack of trust between any two people. It is not our genes to blame, nor the traditional culture. "People were not always like this," my mom once told me, shaking her head slightly. "We used to put all our faith in the course, united and prepared to die for the birth of New China."

Years later, in 1982, when CCP politician Deng Xiaoping assessed the Cultural Revolution (as though someone had to say something to bring closure to it), he described Mao as "seven parts good, three parts bad." Yes, the bad parts have run much deeper and longer. It is a wound that has yet to be healed.

In our family, the scar remained upon the minds of our parents. But my sister, brother, and I have always been close.

My sister was born with a remarkable singing voice. Growing up in the Peking Opera Courtyard, music was in the air all day, and she contributed her part to it. Naturally, before the end of her middle school, she joined the Shenyang Peking Opera Group.

In those years, Peking Opera was the only national art form in Chinese theaters. Jiang Qing (Mao's fourth wife, an actress in her early career) modernized the traditional Peking Opera by creating the "Eight Peking Opera Model Plays." As brilliant as they were in terms of musical and performing arts, they became the only form of entertainment and the most apparent use of propaganda that placed the workers, peasants, and soldiers on center stage.

My sister played key roles in several plays. And our Peking Opera Courtyard became more famous as those fine-looking performers and musicians wore flashier uniforms, made use of stately shuttle buses, and invited envious glances from the people looking on. Nevertheless, I never fancied that my future would have anything to do with Peking Opera.

When my brother was in his first year of middle school, he played Jinghu, the principal instrument in the Peking Opera. Actually, he and I learned it together, as there was nothing else meaningful to do. Two years later, we both auditioned for a junior class in the Shenyang Conservatory of Music and passed the tryouts. My father encouraged my brother to take it, since only one person from each family could be admitted; I had more years available to wait for other opportunities. And I did not have a problem with that decision, anyway.

My sister and brother had each found their life's compass, leaving me the only one in the family with no direction. One day, without me asking, my sister brought someone to coach me to become a news broadcaster, as she said I had an announcer's voice. And my brother had his music friends teach me piano, accordion, and Erhu

(Chinese violin), to find out where my interests and true talents lay. A friend of my father's, a general in the Chinese army, suggested I join the cultural division of the army under his command. But my heart, somehow, was not in any of those things. Quite predictably, by the end of middle school I had only the hamlet life waiting for me.

So, I had now apparently gotten what I deserved, to toil along the endless furrows from sunrise till sunset. At night, I would flip through *People's Literature* and rest up for another ten hours in the field, to prove to the locals—but mostly to myself—that not all city youths were worthless loafers.

The squeaking sound of the door and Secretary Cong's voice jolted me up. "Are you by yourself? Where are the others?" he asked, in a tone of slight disbelief.

I raised my head and saw Secretary Cong and Director Tao enter the room. Every now and then they would check with the host families to inspect our living conditions.

"Out, I guess, playing something," I replied. "Take a seat, please." I gathered my thoughts and gestured to the wood edge of the huokang.

Noticing that I was reading the magazine, Secretary Cong nodded. He was formerly a schoolteacher before being appointed Party Secretary of TianXi. Ma Lin, who was once one of his students, told me all the kids in school were afraid of him.

Half of Secretary Cong's body rested on the edge of the huokang while Director Tao stood beside him. "We handpicked all the host families to make sure you all are safe and well-fed," he said.

"How is everything here?" Director Tao interjected.

"Uncle Liu and Aunt Liu treat us like we are part of the family," I said, which was true.

They both seemed pleased. "You will move into your Youth Center soon," Secretary Cong said. It was exciting news.

He then painted a picture of the as yet unfinished Youth Center. There would be two buildings, with eight rooms in each building. A spacious kitchen would hold two gigantic woks and a deep, indoor well. There would also be an outdoor basketball court and a vegetable garden. Everything would be ready in two months, and that would mark the start of our independent, self-sufficient life.

"There is nothing like it within fifty miles, and most of the peasants will never have seen anything like it!" Secretary Cong stated as he stood up to go. After they both had left the house, I felt reassured that I was on a noble course.

There were many stories about Educated Youths from various places in the country during those years. Either city boys would be destructive among the locals—stealing their chickens, hurting their dogs, and other such things—or the village cadres took advantage of the urban girls and boys by promising them rosy opportunities. Still, whenever I look back on those years, I feel that even though we had come to one of the most impoverished places, we were the blessed ones. We had sensible leaders—Secretary Cong, Director Tao—as well as the caring and good-natured village people.

CHAPTER NINE

AFTER A MONTH OF racing the frost, we finally completed the harvest and distributed the crops among the households. Still, no money changed hands because, after distribution, there were no extra grains to be shipped to the Commune for cash. Nevertheless, harvesting season was still the most electrifying time. We literally tasted the fruits of our labor, and everyone had a few days off. Most of all, we started counting the days until our homecoming as the Chinese New Year drew near.

This was also the time for the annual election of a new Production Unit Captain. At the election meeting, Secretary Cong summarized the year, and then said, "I recommend Wang Cheng to be the Captain for Production Unit 2 in the coming year."

Silence filled the room for a moment, followed by a few people saying, "*Zhong!*" which was their dialect for yes. Secretary Cong had never even discussed it with me, and self-doubt immediately leaped into my head. Which crops could grow better in each field? And how could I learn to tell the time by looking at the sky? The saying 'Newborn calves are not afraid of tigers' would be the only explanation for why I took the job, and a new name, Captain Wang, was heard throughout the village after that day.

In the meantime, another two new girls were recommended for positions. One, GongMein, became an accountant, and another, HuoXing, Women's Director. The three of us had one thing in common—we were to 'eat the bitterness,' which was the very first method to gauge how young people performed during re-education in those years.

HuoXing's father worked under the same Cultural Bureau that my father had for decades. Our similarity in family background and resolve in overcoming hardships drew us closer than with others. The day after I became Captain, HuoXing came to me to lend me her watch, a critical instrument for me to get the labor force out and back each day. "You need it more than I do," she said, her sparkling eyes showing her sincerity.

"I didn't even know you had a watch," I said, surprised. A watch was a valuable personal item in those days.

After we all moved into our Youth Center, I asked Secretary Cong to allow us Sundays off, allowing us time for self-maintenance and to rest our fragile bodies.

"*Zhong*!" Secretary Cong said definitively. "You have come here to learn how to use sickles and hoes," he said, "but more important-ly, your brains need time to grow too." This decision brought back the laughter, the singing, and the basketball matches to our Youth Center—at least for one day a week.

As the end of the year drew nearer, a festive mood took hold within the village, but mostly in the young hearts of the Educated Youths, as we were eager for our first homecoming. While we made no money by sweating on the soil, we could still afford a basket of eggs and a bit of pork to bring home, which were all in severe short-age in Shenyang.

Along with my roommates, I went back to our host family to ask Aunt Liu for the produce. We insisted on paying the retail price for the eggs and meat, which was much higher than the price they would get if they sold it to the Commune Store. Aunt Liu brought out the eggs she had accumulated, and Uncle Liu slaughtered the pig the next day. There was enough meat for the four of us, as well as for their own use.

Coming home to Shenyang for the first time from my 'New Long March,' I felt like a proud soldier returning from the bat-tlefield; or at least, my family made me feel that way, mentioning 'Production Captain Wang' to everyone they knew.

Our family spent a joyous Chinese New Year together, shutting out the craziness from the outside world while making dumplings and savoring the pork and eggs that I'd brought from TianXi. Noth-ing had ever tasted quite so good.

CHAPTER TEN

NINETEEN SEVENTY-SIX WAS a year that altered China's trajectory, and a consequential turning point for several generations, including mine.

January 8 of that year marked the death of Zhou Enlai, who had been the Premier of the State Council of China and the right-hand man of Mao. He was seventy-eight years old. Then, on July 6, Zhu De, the Commander of the People's Liberation Army, who fought alongside Mao for the founding of New China, died at the age of ninety. And most significantly, on September 9, Mao Zedong, the principal founder and leader of the Chinese Communist Party (CCP), and the Chairman of the People's Republic of China, died at eighty-three.

Not coincidentally, almost immediately following on October 6, the Gang of Four (headed by Mao Zedong's widow Jiang Qing, together with Wang Hongwen, Zhang Chunqiao, and Yao Wenyuan) were arrested and detained. The death of Mao and the fall of the Gang of Four, in fact, announced the end of the devastating, decade-long Cultural Revolution—and yet, it all happened without any official declaration. A year before, in 1975, at the recommendation of Mao, Deng Xiaoping had risen for the third time in his political life as the Vice-Chairman of the Central Military Commission, chief of staff of the People's Liberation Army, and Vice Premier of the State Council.

Each of these events were like a meteor striking the earth, rippling out all over China, including to our far-flung, tiny village of TianXi, which had no direct connections to the outside world. In fact, in March 1976, the record shows that a large meteor shower did actually enter the earth's atmosphere. The fiery meteorites peppered over

200 square miles on the outskirts of Jilin City in Northern China. To say it was a fearsome (and coincidental) event was an understatement, especially for a country of one billion people who, although not particularly religious, were very superstitious as a tradition.

These momentous events being what they were, and before any official orders had been issued, the planting season dictated our everyday rituals, as if nothing had happened. As a Captain, I needed to tell the labor force what to do the next day, usually by consulting with Director Tao and my local friend, Ma Lin, beforehand. I got up around 5:00 a.m., grabbed a piece of cornbread, and proceeded to our Production Unit to talk into the speakerphone, listing assigned field locations for that day. I would then carry a long hoe over my shoulder while munching my cornbread, trekking under a dreary sky dotted with dim stars to meet the labor force. Facing the dark, open cornfield, I often felt my thoughts tumbling randomly over one another. It was during one of those moments that the impact of what Mao's departure meant hit me squarely in the face.

For a decade during the Cultural Revolution, a billion people were repeatedly saying, "Long Live Chairman Mao!" Therefore, his death was like the sun that was never supposed to set had just gone down. If we put aside his mishandling of the economy and the failings of the Cultural Revolution, we can see he was undoubtedly an exceptionally inspiring writer and poet, and a distinguished philosopher. Some of his teachings had, in my opinion, noble intentions. Most of the people from that time can still recite his words, even half a century later.

"One is full of vigor; the other is modest and prudent." Those were Mao's words, prescribing how all young people should act. Further enlightening the young, he said, "The world is yours, as well as ours, but ultimately it is yours. Young people are vibrant in the bloom of life, like the sun at eight or nine in the morning. Our hope rests upon all of you." I actually believed in those passages; I tried my best to answer his calling and fulfill his hope.

The next few months whizzed by mostly in routines and boredom. One Sunday, HuoXing ran up to me with the news that a group of people from the Cultural Regiment of Chifeng (the largest city that oversaw the territories, including TianXi) had come to recruit music and performing talents. "They already took me!" she said, panting. "Go for a tryout. You should also make it."

That would have been the best thing during those years for almost anyone—as if a pie had fallen from the sky to land on someone's lap. HuoXing would be free from this rough work in no time to resume a much comfier life in the city while pursuing a singing career. As for me, I had nearly gotten admitted into the Shenyang Conservatory of Music previously. I hadn't taken the opportunity then (or the varied other options I had at the time), and, somehow, I felt I couldn't, or shouldn't, now.

"I'm so happy for you, but I can't go yet," I said to HuoXing. It was not as if I knew what would happen to me—no one could have known. It was more like I had unfinished business, whatever it might be, in TianXi. I went back to my room and found a brand-new diary with a gleaming red cover. I wrote something on the first page and put my name underneath, as I recall. "Wish you all the best." I handed the book to her.

"Thanks!" she said. "Let me know if you ever change your mind."

She took the book, swiftly turning her glittering eyes away before she finished her last words. Watching her back, I stood there with a heavy heart. WuYong had told me he would leave TianXi in two months, as his father had already arranged for him to join the army. Now HuoXing was to leave as well, which was a much bigger surprise for me. It made me think a little more seriously this time: What did my future hold? In those years, no one had a roadmap to follow; thus, fate and serendipity would decide our paths.

CHAPTER ELEVEN

IN TIANXI, WE NEVER worried about starving, albeit we subsisted on a bare minimum of corn for food and cow dung for cooking and heating. Now we lived independently in our Youth Center, and we struggled to get enough cow dung—which we needed a lot of to get through the cold season—let alone bring any money back home for the Chinese New Year. I was seeking solutions to turn things around, or at least to get by for the coming winter.

Since 'Captain Wang' had become a household name in this little rural community, many locals wanted to get closer to me to offer some advice, and I wanted to know as many of them as I could so that I had people to go to for ideas. Director Tao had asked me to his house for a chat over milk tea to let me know he would support me whenever I needed anything. And Ma Lin told me who I could turn to for information for different types of farm work. But none of them could help me with a plan to enhance the Youth Center living conditions.

One day, a man in his mid-forties invited me to his home. Before I became Captain Wang, I had only heard of him being referred to as Old Uncle Zhao, because he hardly ever showed up for work. His slim body, piercing eyes, and pale face were all evident signs that he infrequently worked in the open field. But I heard people often went to him for all kinds of ideas, because he seemed to know about everything and everyone in the vicinity.

His typical mud-walled residence was much neater and more orderly than other local houses. He led me into his room, where a small table sat on top of the huokang. We both sat cross-legged beside the table, where a bottle of *baijiu* and two little cups were already placed. The small flagon of baijiu was inside a larger bowl filled with hot water, just like my father had always done to warm the baijiu before mealtime. Its distinctive, fiery aroma filled the air.

Baijiu, also known as *Shaojiu*, is liquor made from grains. It is typically strong, running around fifty-five to sixty-five percent alcohol content. It tastes fiery on the tongue. Those who could not appreciate baijiu often were seen as less than graceful guests in the eyes of the host.

Uncle Zhao had a teenage daughter, one or two years younger than me, with bright, almond-shaped eyes and two slight dimples on each side of her shy but cheery face. She looked and dressed more like a city girl, although she never uttered a word during that entire evening. I learned that Uncle Zhao also had a son who worked in the Commune Cooperative Store and drew a monthly salary. So now I knew how the bottle of baijiu was purchased, and why Uncle Zhao's daughter dressed as she did.

His daughter brought us a pot of hot milk tea first, and then followed it with two warm plates. The first was piled high with stir-fried eggs: golden, shiny, and wafting a too-long-absent scent into my nose. The other dish was made from fermented Chinese cabbage stew, a typical northeastern Chinese food, as there are no fresh veggies in winter. It tastes much like German sauerkraut, which I recognized later in America. This table of simple food was about as lavish as people here could afford.

Uncle Zhao spoke slowly and often puffed on his pipe and sipped baijiu between statements, as if he were trying to parse through tangled thoughts to pick the right words. "I traveled three or four months a year all alone on a donkey cart to visit friends," Uncle Zhao said. "I received gifts from one friend and passed them on to another along the way. That was how I got to know more people around here than anyone." In those days, things like a brick of tea, homegrown tobacco, a bottle of baijiu, or a piece of sheepskin made grand gifts, and were a great way to make connections.

"TianXi is completely hopeless because of its lack of natural resources, its poor soil, and its distance from any sizeable city to sell agricultural products to a non-agrarian population." The picture he drew of the place we had come to for re-education was a gloomy one.

"I don't see a river or a lake nearby for fishing or irrigation," I added, sounding more like a production captain now.

The only reason that Uncle Zhao had stayed was because he was born and raised in this house and had inherited everything from his parents. He said he would pass this house and its enormous yard on as a dowry for his daughter's wedding when she found the right man.

"If we can ever improve this place," he said, "we will need to take loans from the Commune, or from factories in Shenyang, to buy a few tractors. Then we can let machines do the farming to free up labor for side-businesses that make money." Half of a bottle baijiu later, I was in the clouds, reveling in a lovely, if fictitious, image of TianXi.

During those years, thinking about getting rich was as bad as committing a robbery; thus, you would not hear this kind of talk from any official media, not even fictional works. "That was capitalism, the root for all the evils, and it was like flood and beast," were Mao's words. Was Mao completely wrong, I wondered?

So that was a different type of lesson that I got from a true peasant. Not the way our re-education was intended to be, obviously.

At last, Uncle Zhao mentioned that Secretary Cong wanted to send a local peasant to live in our Youth Center to make sure nothing unfortunate would happen to us. And he was willing to do it.

"As far as I'm concerned, Uncle Zhao is the right person for us," I said when Secretary Cong sought my opinion on the local representative a few days later.

When I later reflected on my situation, I realized that if the Cultural Revolution had lasted for a few more years, Uncle Zhao and I might have grown much closer, and TianXi might even have become my permanent home. Many Educated Youths married local girls and settled in the countryside. What if that had happened to me? That weird but not-unlikely circumstance sometimes crossed my mind even decades later. But back then, our destinies were never in our own hands.

After Secretary Cong assigned Uncle Zhao as the local representative to live with us, I asked him if there could be a way to better our life in the Youth Center. He puffed on his pipe a few times before responding. "If we could use the truck coming from Shenyang to transport a truckload of raw salt from further north in Inner-Mongolia at a dirt-cheap price…" He puffed the pipe again. "Then we could easily turn it into substantial money."

Often trucks from Shenyang arrived to deliver building supplies.

And out here, salt was rare, but one thing that every household needed year-round.

"Let me consult Secretary Cong." I could not wait to propose this idea.

"Zhong!" Secretary Cong agreed with his usual assertiveness after a moment's thought. "There is a girl in your center whose father is a general manager at a major factory in Shenyang. A truck from his factory will come soon. I will ask her father, as a favor, to have the driver accompany you and Zhao on the trip." The cost would be only a few extra barrels of gasoline, which was nothing for a state-owned factory.

A few days later, I heard that the general manager had happily agreed. My dimmed, empty heart suddenly brightened with a meaningful goal. I became excited again and looked forward to turning our living conditions around.

There was an Inner-Mongolia salt lake about 500 miles away, near the border with Siberia of Soviet Russia. There was no road—only hilly, barren land, which was icy this late in October. But I was like a newborn calf, unfazed by the tiger. I thought that if Uncle Zhao said we could make the trip, as he had on a donkey cart once before, then we would be fine. When the truck arrived, and after two days of preparation, the three of us—the driver, whom we called Master Li, Uncle Zhao, and me—were ready to leave on our expedition.

CHAPTER TWELVE

IT SEEMED PRETTY STRAIGHTFORWARD. The standard military truck, brand-named 'Grand Liberation,' was overall quite solid. Master Li was a quiet, vigorous man, an ex-soldier who had driven for twenty years in the army. And he was determined to carry on this duty for the daughter of his general manager. Most of all, we had Uncle Zhao to go with us.

It was a cloudless, autumnal day in late October, and the crisp air was scented with earthy aromas which rendered an intoxicating, rich bouquet. Equipped with a heavy sheepskin overcoat, a bulky bomber hat, and steel-toed boots—I'm not sure where my mom found them for me, but she had sent them with her latest package—I could hardly contain my exhilaration. Once again, my mind soared like a bird winging its way out of its cage and into the sky.

The first day on the road went by fast. Before we knew it, the golden sun was right above the western horizon. Our Grand Liberation had already pressed far into the Mongolian ethnic region.

"Let me talk to the people, to see if we can spend a night there." Uncle Zhao said, his pipe pointing to a large Mongolian ger that had a few smaller ones surrounding it. These large, portable tents were made of sheep or cow skins and wooden slats, just enough to protect nomadic families from the merciless weather conditions of the region.

Master Li and I followed Uncle Zhao to the ger. After a few knocks, a man in a long robe with a dark red, weather-beaten face and a knife hanging on his waist opened the door. It was impossible to guess his age, because his agile movements contradicted his noticeably-aged skin. Uncle Zhao said a few words I did not understand. Our host bent his back, and his one hand hinted for us to enter.

Once inside, Uncle Zhao brought out a brick of tea wrapped with old, yellow paper and a bottle of baijiu from his pocket. They both bowed toward one another, as if they had rehearsed the entire scene countless times. A lady wearing a colorful apron stood in the shadows as she wrapped her hair in a knot. She fanned the fire in a stove with a big pot on top of it. After sitting cross-legged on several pieces of sheepskin, we reached for our tobacco pouches and rolled our cigarettes. For me, this ritual was more to fill the silence than to satisfy a tobacco craving.

The golden sun turned orange-red, and then completely dropped off the horizon. Inside the ger was dim, but not yet dark enough to light an oil lantern. Flickering light from the flames in the stove danced upon the wall, radiating warmth all around. The smell of burning cow dung filled the ger.

Before long, the lady presented a steaming bowl of milk tea to each of us. A single sip of the hot milk tea instantly thawed the chill in me, and as we grew accustomed to our surroundings, our demure hostess set up another stove at the center of the room. She placed a wok on top of it and added water. She moved so quietly that we barely noticed her at work.

While Uncle Zhao spoke his broken Mongolian to the host, Master Li and I chatted about how far we had to go—two more days to reach the lake, if things progressed as smoothly as they had today.

The evening slipped into darkness. The oil lamp was lit and shone its soft light all around the room. The water in the wok started to boil, and the lady added pieces of mutton to it. I felt hungry.

Our host passed each of us a knife; he used his to stir the mutton in the wok. He picked up a sizeable piece of the meat, carved off a small part of it, dipped it on a salt plate, and dropped it into his mouth. He raised his chin to indicate to us to do the same.

This single course of the meal was famously known as 'hand-held mutton' in Inner-Mongolia, and later all over the country. While we sliced and ate, and downed the baijiu, the lady kept adding fresh pieces into the wok. It was such a simple way of preparing a meal, yet the natural flavor from the fresh mutton would be difficult to duplicate anywhere else.

Uncle Zhao and Master Li were both travelers, which made them good drinkers, too. My father had passed his drinking ritual on to me, and it seemed that there was no better time to put it to use than now. We hardly made conversation, but always followed the host whenever he raised his bowl of baijiu. (Ethnic Mongolians are known to be drinkers; they drink it from rice bowls and have no formality whatsoever.) The movements of knives in and out of the steaming wok filled both the time and our stomachs, while our alcohol intake went well beyond our natural, circumscribed boundaries.

A rooster crowing awakened me. My eyes were blinded by the sun's rays peeking through the skylight of the ger. No one seemed to remember when we had fallen asleep the night before, but we thanked our host and took to the road without delay. For the next few hours I learned a few things from Uncle Zhao about Mongolian customs.

Most Mongolians believe in Lamaism, a form of Buddhism taught and maintained by Lamas in Tibet. The Naadam Festival (the "recreation festival" in Mongolian) is an annual festival that has been held for centuries, usually in the summer, when the sun-kissed prairie was most fertile. The festival lasted seven days, with people from all over Inner-Mongolia attending it. Wrestling, horse-racing, and archery were the central draws of the festival, along with dancing and singing—not to mention a day and a night of binge eating and drinking.

Mongolians are incredibly humble, if not being threatened by nature or enemies, and amicable toward strangers. That one night in the ger was enough to convince me that they were a people born with laudable virtues. Most of them, I learned, had no formal education because of their nomadic lifestyle lived mostly on horseback.

In contrast, Han Chinese made up more than ninety percent of the Chinese population. What were our core traditions and beliefs? Even Confucian teachings, which rested on three essential values— filial piety, humaneness, and ritual—had been completely repudiated by Mao. And Communism? How could the Chinese be expected to grasp even the basic principles of this exotic ideology—even for its ninety million strong CCP members—and incorporate it into our mythos and folklore?

I was baffled then, and I am still pondering it now.

CHAPTER THIRTEEN

OUR GRAND LIBERATION PENETRATED northward on the grassy, muddy, wobbly terrain. Gloomy clouds formed over the hills on the northern horizon and closed in upon us as the temperature steadily dropped. With it dropped my cheery mood. However, with our higher purpose in mind, we were no less driven than the Grand Liberation.

The clouds grew thicker and darker, releasing raindrops mixed with sleet that beat on the windshield. Grand Liberation was chugging along, unfazed, but roaring louder at a slower pace. The road, such as it was, quickly became treacherous. A frown appeared on Master Li's face as he tightened his grip on the steering wheel, revving the engine like ominous music in a horror movie.

"How bad is it, Master Li?" I could not help but ask.

"*TaMaDe*! How do I know; I have never been here before!" The curse words, akin to 'damn it,' leaped from his mouth. His face twisted in rage. "But there is no place to stop anyway." He wasn't done venting. "I was a military driver for twenty years and drove through all kinds of conditions, but never in such a shitty situation. In those years, before any major movement, a scout team would have gone in first to check the roads."

"We forgot to ask your general manager to send a scout." Uncle Zhao maintained his usual sense of wit. He had come this way once, as he sometimes related, by himself on a donkey cart. The trip had taken him three months. He usually stayed in one place for two or three days to be sure about the weather and to plan his next move. He'd had to deal with harsh weather many times but he'd made it through. Of course, we wanted to come back within a week, which left no time to wait for better weather. "Don't follow the cart track;

it will become muddy with the rain," Uncle Zhao suggested. "The flat land with dry grass is firmer to drive on."

Before Master Li could steer the truck out of the muddy tracks, the seats underneath us suddenly sank about a foot; then we were not moving at all, even as the vroom of the engine grew louder with each attempt to rock the vehicle free from the mud. All to no avail. "TaMaDe, that's it!" Master Li sounded more deflated than irate.

"At least this is not a donkey cart." Uncle Zhao was still upbeat. I agreed. We had the metal cabin, plus enough food and water.

The rain had developed into snow as temperatures dropped below freezing. We had seen a few gers about forty-five minutes ago, now fifteen miles behind us. We knew that sitting inside the truck would do us no good, so we decided that Uncle Zhao and I would go to find help while Master Li stayed with Grand Liberation.

CHAPTER FOURTEEN

FOR THE FIRST HOUR, walking in the snow was truly mesmerizing. Staying behind Uncle Zhao, I fixated my eyes on each upcoming step to make sure I did not accidentally slip into a pit. After a while in those unsettling surroundings, time seemed to stand still. We became the only two people in the universe. Our heavy shoes squeezed the snow beneath us, both rhythmical and hypnotic.

My thoughts drifted to a parallel scene from my mom's childhood, when she was a schoolgirl walking along a goat trail through the mountains on her way to middle school. My mom's family lived in Yongding County, Fujian Province, in a secluded Hakka village nestled deep in the mountains. "There was no middle school in Yongding County," my mom had told me. "We had to walk for two days, over forty kilometers on mountainous goat trails, to a middle school in nearby DaPu County. Usually, my brother, three cousins, and I walked together, plus three family porters who accompanied us.

"As we grew older," my mom went on, "we would march to school in one day— ten hours without stopping. Our three porters would each shoulder a pole that bore two baskets filled with food and supplies for us at the boarding school. The porters came once a month to bring us more essentials."

Trudging over the trails several times a year during her six years of middle school and high school accounted for many of my mom's memories of her adolescent years. Until she finished high school, she was raised in one of the most renowned Tulou (earthen castles) in China. Her grandfather had designed, built, and named it Zhencheng Lou (Castle of Revitalization).

My great grandfather was a successful businessman, trading tobacco in Xiamen and Shanghai. He put the profits into building

Zhencheng Lou, just as the leaves of a 100-foot tree always fall toward its roots. He had all the building materials shipped from Shanghai, some of which took several months to reach the village. The castle has four stories, with 222 rooms in total. As a fortified castle it looks rustic and medieval from the outside, but stately on the inside, famously blending Eastern and Western styles. The castle took five years to build and seven years to decorate—all being completed in 1912. A lustrous plaque fashioned by my great grandfather still hangs above the grand entrance today.

Years later, in 2008, Zhencheng Lou and a few others in Fujian were inscribed by UNESCO as a cluster of World Cultural Heritage Sites for their exceptional architecture, Hakka wisdom, and the communal living of that solitary environment. Many of my mom's relatives still live in Zhencheng Lou today while keeping its grand central courtyard and other major sections open for public exhibitions.

My mother's family is Hakka, a sub-group of the Han ethnic group that makes up ninety-one percent of the Chinese population. Her family tree goes back hundreds of years, although it records men's names only. "Women were married out to other villages, so what was the point?" Mom observed.

Hakkas are known for having originated as a migratory people. They distinguish themselves by two criteria: you have Hakka blood, and you can speak the Hakka language. This second condition made the rest of our family complete strangers when we gathered with my mom's parents, brothers, and sisters because they all spoke Hakka about their family affairs.

Despite their insular nature, they never forgot about the outside world or stopped dreaming about the future. Generation by generation, they raised their children to transcend their parents. The children would be sent overseas for the best education, although they never forgot their humble roots. My mom's brother, who walked to school with her on the mountain trails, became the Academician of the Chinese Academy of Sciences. Her other siblings are in America, England, Taiwan, Hong Kong, and other places outside Mainland China.

Similar to my mother's experience, TianXi was remote, solitary, and devoid of most essentials. And yet most villagers, nor their children, ever ventured beyond where their donkey carts could reach.

"The benevolent love the mountains; the wise love the water." Confucius said this 2,500 years ago, and the axiom has confounded people ever since. Trudging through the snow, contemplating my mother and her people, the saying reverberated in my head clearer than ever before. Surely, Confucius was implying that those who loved mountains (and land) would stay there for life, while those who loved water would travel, multiplying their wisdom. His insight could, in part, distinguish the people who chose TianXi, and those who migrated like the Hakkas.

Realizing I had inherited the enigmatic and potent Hakka gene from my mom made me feel proud and humbled all at once—I was tougher for it, and yet not nearly as strong as true Hakka people, my mom included. My mom's family history struck me that Hakkas are more Chinese than most Chinese known to the world. However, some of their dispositions tend to spark animosities toward the non-Hakka Chinese people. Such cultural divisions prevail in many cultures throughout the world.

Decades later, I visited Zhencheng Lou. Ah Jun, the son of my mom's cousin, led me in and out, around this legendary mud castle for two full days. I met a dozen close relatives living in Zhencheng Lou that day and savored homemade food, rice wine, teas, and fruits. I then immersed myself in the family museum. A roomful of photos show Hakka's history and our extended family going back hundreds of years. In recent years, many scholars and top CCP (Chinese Communist Party) leaders, including Xi Jinping, have visited Hakka Tulou. They did not come to deepen their political dogmas but to grasp Hakka's true essence.

It should come as no surprise when scholars have suggested that those who have a profound interest in the Chinese revolution should delve into the secrecies of the Hakkas. Their character traits have forged many influential leaders in modern history. Son Yet Sen, Deng Xiaoping, Lee Kuan Yew, Hu Yaobang, Zhu De, Chen Yi, Guo Moruo, among many others, have one thing in common: Hakka roots.

"We have water from this deep well," Ah Jun pointed to the big, dark hole on the stone-paved ground, "plus enough grain and dried vegetables in storage. We could close the gate for two years without going hungry. We have enough stored to feed eighty people."

I nodded in admiration.

"Come back again and live here with us for a week or two. I will prepare a room for you and tell you more stories about us," Ah Jun said to me at the doorstep.

"I will," I responded enthusiastically.

CHAPTER FIFTEEN

FINALLY, UNCLE ZHAO AND I found those gers sitting in the twilight and surrounded by an eerie quiet. My body, warm after hours of brisk walking, shivered a little. We realized this place had been deserted for quite some time.

I followed Uncle Zhao to the door of the largest ger, and he pushed the hanging rug open. The rug fell off, stirring up a cloud of dust and the smell of mildew. I squeezed my body inside through the narrow doorway, only to meet more of the suffocating smell. In the dim light, I saw a few sheepskins piled on top of hay loosely spread over the ground. A pile of mud in the center that held half-burned cow dung appeared to once have been a stove. After a little while, my nose and eyes adjusted to the surroundings.

"This place is your latest new home, Xiao Wang," Uncle Zhao said, using his endearment for me, "for a *higher* level of re-education." (In China, an elderly person often refers to a much younger person as 'Xiao' followed by his or her last name once they become close.)

"Looks like the vastness of nature will be my teacher this time, but I wish it could cook me some warm cornbread and vegetable soup," I said, thinking of the hot meal we'd shared on our first day with my host family in TianXi.

Uncle Zhao started to make repairs on the degraded mud stove, and I found a broken basket for collecting cow dung. Although it was dark, the gleaming snow under the dull sky magnified all surrounding objects. I kicked things around on my way, like I used to as a little kid, looking for small treasures buried in the snow. This time, my search was for survival.

Before long, I'd collected enough to get us through the night. Uncle Zhao had the fire started already. It was close to midnight. We put a few pieces of cornbread on the side of the stove and brought out bottles of water. I had never before experienced such a feeling of being a castaway.

"Last time I came this way by myself, on a donkey cart." Uncle Zhao was in a reminiscent mood. It was a perfect time and place to tell his story. His pipe hurled out a pungent scent, which penetrated my nose and eyes. As my first line of defense, I pulled out my tobacco pouch to roll one of my own. I could handle it better if I smoked at the same time.

After raising his thin pipe several times, he continued: "I got stuck in a place for five days because one wheel fell off the cart..." His eyes twinkled as he painstakingly revealed the events long kept in his memory, as if he were unfolding an old canvas painting, afraid of causing more creases.

Apparently, on the second day by himself, Uncle Zhao ran out of food and resorted to digging into a bag of the donkey's feed, to which he added some raw sorghum. Throughout my childhood memory, as much as we were deprived of most foods, I thought even the most processed sorghum was only fit for cattle. My mom often liked to tell our family guests that whenever we had sorghum porridge for lunch, I would hide under the table, pretending to have a stomachache.

I'm not sure how late we stayed up as Uncle Zhao recounted these and other stories—not that it mattered anyway. Eventually, I gathered some loose hay and buttoned my sheepskin overcoat, ready to slip into a dream. "The hardest part," Uncle Zhao's voice lingered in my head, "was not eating the raw sorghum mixed with hay, because that caused constipation for a week, it was the time that I ran out of tobacco and used corn leaves instead—that was simply awful!" The way he said it, I knew he truly meant it.

I could not tell whether I actually slept, as the images that floated through my head—a blend of Uncle Zhao's last trip and this one—played repeatedly, mixed with the sounds of coyotes or wolves howling in the distance.

Unlike the American wild west, in the vastness of the Inner-Mongolian upland where Khans had once roamed, there were no bandits, and no stories about them as far as I could recall. Many indigenous people had guns, of course, and everyone carried waist knives, but these were only used against nature. How this harsh living environment had nurtured the kindest and most generous people on earth was beyond me.

I awoke to a whiff of burning cow dung. Uncle Zhao had already set a fire against the freezing morning. I rubbed my sleepy eyes and dragged myself out of my warm hay nest. I looked through the open doorway to see outside. A vast, silver blanket covered the entire landscape, so bright I had to squint. Snow was falling; it was as if we were in a beautiful painting as a master's hand leisurely made the finishing strokes. I withdrew from the door and approached the stove to find Uncle Zhao using a broken ceramic bowl to heat water from snow.

"What is the boiling water for?" I asked.

"I have brought a small bag of stir-fried corn flour with me," Uncle Zhao said. "Mixing it with boiling water will be our meal. Eating one meal a day, we should be good for three days."

Eating raw sorghum on his last trip seemed to have taught him a valuable lesson. "Lucky me!" I muttered.

Chapter Sixteen

Being stuck in the deserted ger allowed me more free time than I'd had since I first set out on my New Long March. And after we trekked deep into Inner-Mongolia, there were no political slogans to be seen, which further reinforced my sense of being a castaway. It was mesmerizing and serene. I felt that only a lone bird, free in the pure vastness of the sky, could feel this way. The nomadic lifestyle was simple, even primitive, and free from human influences.

So, why were slogans and indoctrinations filling our society and shaping our minds? I did not understand. If a bird wanted to remain happily as a bird, then why force it to become an eagle?

Nothing seemed to bother Uncle Zhao, though, as he sat cross-legged like a Buddha by the fire. His stern face, covered by road dust and a layer of soot from cow dung ashes, was lit by the orange glow of the fire. He seemed wholly drawn into the flickering flames, puffing on his pipe nonstop. I was sure he was calculating something, which comforted me.

The third morning, when I pushed the re-attached hanging rug open, I heard a familiar sound approaching from the distance. It was our Grand Liberation! I hurried in to get Uncle Zhao. We both came out, our four arms in the air, waving to Master Li.

Amazingly, he had driven the truck out of that hole. When he had warmed the engine that morning, he'd noticed that the ground was firmer now that the snow had halted for a day. He released the air from the tires trapped in the mud and found a few pieces of deadwood to put underneath the flats to create more traction. He then replaced the flat tires with the spares, and the Grand Liberation was ready to roar again.

We finally reached our destination, a vast lake completely blanketed for as far as the eye could see by a layer of dusty brown, raw salt. It was free so long as we shoveled the salt ourselves onto the truck. And we did, a full day of hard labor for a truckload of valuable salt.

Five days later, our Grand Liberation—and the three of us covered in a thick layer of sweat, road dust, and raw salt that made us hardly recognizable—rumbled back into TianXi. For those ten days, we had never taken off our shoes and overcoats, seldom washing our faces and hands. But we were home, unharmed, and in high spirits. Mission accomplished!

"I was so worried; I couldn't sleep for days!" Secretary Cong exclaimed, his face beaming with delight, yet mostly relief, to see us return safely. During the last ten days, no one could tell where we were, let alone guess what could have happened to us. "I regretted letting you all go just to pick up a truckload of salt."

"I have more fear thinking about it now," I admitted to Secretary Cong. "I mean, what if the truck had broken down, or one of us had gotten sick? We are truly fortunate to have accomplished our task and made it home safely."

I was speechless seeing the excited faces in our Youth Center, who had counted the days since we'd left. They came to hug and congratulate me. My childhood friend WuYong cooked me egg noodle soup, with four big, golden eggs in the steaming pot!

During the following months, donkey carts came to our center in droves, their drivers hoping to buy salt at a low price—even lower than from the government-owned cooperative stores. It was our way to show our gratitude to the villagers. And before the end of the year, everyone in the Youth Center had seventy yuan in their pockets, equivalent to a two-month worker's wage in Shenyang. For most, it was the most money we'd ever had, and it was also my first taste of capitalism (there was nothing evil about it, as we had been taught to believe). Instead, it conveyed a sense of reward realized by our hard labor.

Chapter Seventeen

As the Cultural Revolution abruptly fizzled out, so too did my youthful aspirations. It was something like a long-term patient in a mental institution who had suddenly recuperated and discovered the fanciful world he had distantly known was really a vague, absurd one. Suddenly, sweating it out on the furrows had lost all meaning, and every day now felt like a year. I was dying on the inside but still could not decide which might be worse: leaving TianXi to do something I had no interest in doing, or hanging around the remote village in perpetual despair. I visited Uncle Zhao more frequently, bringing with me canned food that my mom had sent to supplement his baijiu. Our salt trip, plus strong white liquor, had bonded us. Besides, unlike Secretary Cong, he never lectured me.

"I know you won't stay in TianXi forever, but you all have one of two ways to leave," Secretary Cong once told us. "Either you will feel sorry for having been here, or you will feel proud for the rest of your life at what you have learned and accomplished." I had never felt sorry for coming to TianXi, although toward the end of my stay I was not so sure. That made Uncle Zhao the perfect person to confide in—someone with whom I could seek counsel in a lively chat over hard liquor.

One day, after a little too much drinking the night before, I overslept. Secretary Cong came to check on me. Seeing me still in bed, reeking of alcohol, he pulled my blanket over on me and left without a word. I would rather have heard harsh words from him; ones that would inflict sharp pain, but would still make me less miserable than the deeper, dull pain of guilt. I had let him and the people of TianXi down. And more than any time in the past, I had let myself down. Yet, two days later, when melancholy descended over me, I found myself at Uncle Zhao's door all over again.

"You are right on time, Xiao Wang." Uncle Zhao was as easy-going as usual. "My son just brought some leftover stir-fried tofu from the Commune Collective Store." He was taking out a lunchbox from several layers of wrappings. The wrappings were newspapers.

"May I have those newspapers?" The wrappings, more than the food, drew my attention. They were only a few days old, I'd noticed, topical news that could only be found at the Commune Center.

"Sure, but they're not a grand idea for your toilet business, unless you want to smarten up your butt with black ink." He never passed up a chance to be witty. "Trust me, all-natural cornstalk leaves are better for that."

His joke drew a pleasant chuckle from me. That was true, even for us city youngsters. Few people could take half a day to go to the Commune Collective store to buy toilet paper, so everyone was taking care of business differently; cornstalk leaves, as the most accessible, were not an unacceptable option, I admitted.

Thinking back on those years in TianXi, corn was practically the third essential substance for life—right after air and water. Corn kernels were food staples, the stalks were used for cooking and heating, its husks as insoles for shoes and toilet paper—no part of the corn plant was wasted. However, when I visited decades later, even this edge-of-the-earth place had changed. The people had burned all the cornstalks, because they now had no use for them. Secretary Cong, who had greeted me at the train station with a "Welcome home!" that warmed my heart, told me, "Two households can produce more grains now than the whole TianXi Production Team when you were here." And every household now had tap water and radiator heaters inside their homes. When I had lived there, survival was the first and only instinct for us all. And I was learning that physical survival wasn't the only kind that was important. "Please keep those newspapers for me whenever you have them. I will stop by to collect them." I sensed that something big was about to happen in the country.

Reading these newspapers helped me to connect the dots of everything that had happened far beyond TianXi. After the death of Mao in 1976, which signaled the end of the Cultural Revolution, Deng Xiaoping, the Vice Premier, officially presided over the State

Council's daily work. The first thing Deng realized was that the national education system, which had been paralyzed for an alarming eleven years, required a severe wake-up call. This news caused a faint stirring within me, slowly waking me up to the fact that numbing myself with baijiu only sank me into a deeper hole. I had never felt this feeble and lonesome before, desperately needing someone to talk to. HuoXing's final words to me crept into my head. "Let me know if you ever change your mind." They conjured memories of how her distinct voice had always cheered me up in the past. "I'm sure I have lost my mind," I mumbled to myself, "which made it even more necessary to contact her."

I knew only that the Cultural Regiment where she worked was in Chifeng, and it took a day-and-half to get there by donkey cart, bus, and then by train. It was near the end of the year, and the busy farming season was already over, so this was a perfect time to get away for a few days.

"I'd like to take four days off to visit Chifeng City, maybe to clear my head," I said to Secretary Cong, expecting to hear his agreement. He did not even look at me. "I will arrange a donkey cart tomorrow to take you to the bus station near the Commune Center." He uttered his response without raising his head from his accounting book. In my eagerness to see HuoXing, and also to get out of my rut, I was on the road again. I brought with me a small basket of eggs for her—the only thing from TianXi that had any value.

There was no telephone I could use to tell her I was coming. So when I arrived, I was told her Regiment was away on a performing tour. I had no choice but to leave the basket of eggs and a brief note on her desk. I took another train back to TianXi, feeling utterly deflated. I had done nothing but chase my own shadow. I was ready to capitulate: maybe TianXi was my true destiny.

Decades later, when HuoXing and I reconnected in Shenyang, we both knew what my spontaneous but mistimed visit to her in Chifeng had meant. We chatted and laughed as if we had never parted. Neither of us brought up the hypothetical—what if I had found her in Chifeng and we had reconnected back then? We have both long accepted the life that fate has dealt us. We have remained close friends ever since—although it is unlike many Hollywood screenplays, it is better this way. Actual lives flow more like a gentle stream, as opposed to the torrent experienced for two hours sitting in a theater.

I stood and reached up to the luggage rack for the bottle of baijiu that I'd brought in my bag for the lengthy train ride. Still holding the bag in my hand, I noticed a few young people curled over books or notepads, writing. Two of them, looking like a father and son, sat across the aisle from me. The younger held a book so close to his near-sighted glasses, it was as if no one else existed in the world. This scene had been foreign to me growing up—no one had ever showed any interest in books; not openly and in public, at least.

"*Nihao.*" I approached the older man courteously. "Is he your son? He seems so absorbed in his reading!"

"Yes, he is my son." Holding a cup of tea, he took a sip and continued. "Deng Xiaoping has just announced the reopening of all the universities and the resumption of GaoKao. Being a middle school teacher, I am finally going back to work, and I want my son to go to college, so he is preparing for GaoKao."

The annual, nationwide college admission examination, famously known as GaoKao, had disappeared for more than a decade. Suddenly, like the single brightest star in the sky, its reappearance had captured the attention of everyone in the country. The man's eyes lit up, full of longing for himself and his son. It was as if the bleakest and most prolonged winter had finally ended. Seeing me in the right age group, the schoolteacher added, "You might as well try to get into college, too." He pushed up his nearsighted glasses habitually. "Have you thought of it?"

After a long pause, I replied, "I am not certain I could make it, even though the college doors are now open." I placed the bag back onto the luggage rack, including the bottle of baijiu, and sat down in silence to weigh the schoolteacher's advice. I liked the idea of GaoKao. Perhaps I had stumbled onto something that I had been yearning for all along without knowing it.

CHAPTER EIGHTEEN

COMING BACK TO TIANXI from my disappointing but not futile trip, I sensed my path might one day take a sharp turn, although now it looked only like a distant sparkle. To make the college dream come true, one must pass the stringent admission test, beating out ninety-five percent of all other applicants.

The unexpected announcement that the annual GaoKao would resume in 1977 revived the hopes of more than just college-aged people. Everyone sensed the drastic shift of the sentimental Feng Qi, this time in a far more positive way than the Revolution.

The term "Feng Qi" has a broad and distinct meaning in Chinese. I have been wrestling to find a concise English counterpart that is also rich and versatile enough in its implications. The term comprises two graphic characters: Feng, which means wind, and Qi, which is air. When putting the two together, people who know some Chinese can intuit what this implies. "Cultural weather" could be a simplistic and quite literal interpretation, but Feng Qi can be used in other respects as well. It often suggests a sudden and most obvious shift in the strong emotional, social, cultural, political, or overall moral trend.

Considering that China has the largest population in the world, the people of the entire country are surprisingly like-minded; this is mostly because only one dominant ethnic group has lived in its closed system almost since its beginnings. Thus, any change in Feng Qi could sway the mood of more than one billion people one way or another. When the top leaders in China exert their power to influence society, usually by announcement—as they have many times in the past—the people have been able to sense the shift of Feng Qi to indicate what new direction is being embraced and try to figure out what it might mean for them personally.

By September of 1977, the recommencement of the annual Ga-oKao had turned Feng Qi around by 180 degrees. It appeared on the headlines of all the newspapers first, and then became the daily conversation of everyone, everywhere. It suddenly seemed that the *glorious models* that were established during the Cultural Revolution were merely a temporary diversion, and the intellectuals took back the institutes, and the teachers returned to their classrooms.

However, the situation looked anything but reassuring. The college-aged population had been growing each year for more than a decade, and most of them had been dispersed across the countryside, having nowhere else to go. During those years, many college facilities were severely neglected, the faculties having left the campus to receive re-education. Such factors elevated the college threshold higher than at any time in the past, and getting into a college was only a dream for most college-aged people. As for myself, I had learned next to nothing during my elementary and middle school years, which were precisely in parallel with the ten years of the Cultural Revolution. Yet, for the first time in my life, I wanted to follow my heart.

"I'd like to step down as the Production Captain to prepare for GaoKao." I laid out the simple desire to Secretary Cong. Everyone had heard of GaoKao, even in the forever unstirred TianXi.

"Zhong," the most pleasing tone emanated from Secretary Cong again, "you should go for it!" His supportive stance was more than I had expected, marking this as one of my most memorable impressions of him.

He asked me to continue to oversee our youth affairs, which was a far easier task, but it meant I had to stay in TianXi, where candlelight was more reliable than electric bulbs, while I studied for GaoKao. And more particularly, facing the ocean of knowledge between my current reality and my ideal future, where should I start?

Looking back on my educational footprints as far as I could remember, I had almost nothing to show for it. I suddenly realized that "Educated Youth" was merely a cultural label—in reality, "educated" was a huge overstatement for most of us who were sent to the countryside. The reasons had been political and social, but also economic; as it was later revealed, one of the harsh realities facing the central government was that there were no jobs for those sixteen million young people in urban areas during that ten-year time period.

In my case, I could not recall the name of even one of my Chinese language teachers even though Chinese literature was the only subject I'd loved. Worse yet, I did not remember ever having to take a math test during my middle school years; at the time, I always thought I had dodged a bullet, but now I searched my memory to understand what had happened, and I realized that an essential element was missing in my childhood—basic education. What had happened?

Of all my education thus far (education was compulsory only for the nine years of elementary and middle school back then), I had spent my last three years of elementary school in Daqing, and four years for middle school in Shenyang. I was as happy as any school kid could be, yet all that time I had done little toward becoming a truly "educated youth," because no such dream had presented itself.

By the end of my third year in Daqing Commune, I was sent back to Shenyang to go to a middle school by myself while my family was still in Daqing. For one year, I sojourned with Wu Yong's family, as our parents were lifelong friends.

Although that school was reputed to be one of the best in the city, we spent more time outside the school. Every other month, our entire class of forty-five students would go to a nearby factory or commune to purify our young thoughts. Our teacher, who led us on the trips, would try to teach us something during breaks, but no one paid much attention. We were led to believe knowledge was at best useless, and at worst harmful, to a young soul.

Today, we can all trace our traumatic experiences back to those moments that have lingered even many decades later. Just like a red-hot iron pressed against the hide of a cow, the brand does not fade with time. For many Chinese people, the marked effects of the Cultural Revolution are like scars burned into our brains, scars that even tend to pass through generations.

The first of these scars is a lack of trust. There is a popular saying now in twenty-first century China for when a person asks a friend to borrow some money: the friend might say, "I would rather lend you my other half."

Mao firmly believed that "Regime comes out of the guns." But he did not stop the revolution after the takeover of China and instead launched the Cultural Revolution. Although there were no guns, radical politics divided the country—and even families—by labeling people into two classes: bourgeoisie and proletariat. Since then, 'class struggle' has become, and remains, a dominating theme.

In the post-Mao era, this social rift has grown into a subtler, but more profound phenomenon: aloofness between people. It is present between almost any two people. For instance, when you go to a restaurant in China and the waitress comes to you with a stern face, do not take it personally. Emotional distancing was—and still is—a norm within the country.

Personality worship also took root during the Mao era, and it still exists in the post-Mao period today. Somehow, it has grown into a form of flattery, a quite prominent part of the culture today. Many pride themselves for having this social skill, a delicate way to please one's superiors. Obsequious words can be heard in almost every conversational exchange, from ordinary people up to the top, with a reckless disregard for truthfulness.

Decades later, when I visited China and met up with my college friends, one commented, "The way you talk, you can't survive in China, Wang Cheng." I knew what he meant, having no current sense of this social skill. I realized that I had perhaps become a bit too Americanized to fit into the present-day Chinese culture. In the U.S., we all refer to one another by our first names, whether at work or in social life, regardless of one's pay grade, management level, or what kind of car one drives.

In China, however, if you leave out the job title on the last name of your senior officer—in writing or in conversation, on formal or casual occasions—then you should be ready for a poor performance review and to have to update your résumé. In life, being honest and truthful, which is synonymous to a lack of social skills, is one sure way to derail you from developing social bonds.

Truly, the Chinese culture was revolutionized during the ten years between 1966 and 1976. Yet to what effect, I still remain more than a little puzzled.

CHAPTER NINETEEN

The news of college reopening to all the people—although mostly those from ages sixteen to twenty-eight—was released with more details. The first resumed annual GaoKao would take place over three days, on December 7, 8 and 9, 1977, leaving only three months for all us hopefuls to prepare for it. Under normal circumstances, the annual GaoKao always took place in summer followed with fall college admissions. Nineteen seventy-seven was anything but normal. The country, as Deng put it, could not afford the dysfunctional education system to continue any longer.

The possibility of going to college—a once-in-a-lifetime opportunity—presented me with the most daunting challenge I had ever considered; I had no book knowledge to rely on to leap over this intimidating gulf.

Did I have anything to show for my formative years? I searched my childhood memories to see what might emerge, but I could not recall even one time that my parents had directed me. This was quite unlike most of my friends' parents, who guided their children at every turn.

My closest friend, WuYong, joined the army after his first year in TianXi, as arranged by his father. HuoXing left TianXi to become a singer, succumbing to her father's nagging. In comparison, my parents let me decide everything for myself. They supported me regardless of the choices I made. Perhaps it was because I had never asked them. Or perhaps they thought it would work out best for me that way. And maybe it was more complicated than that.

By the time I was sent to TianXi, people like my parents had very little self-confidence left after being labeled as "the bourgeoisie." "We should do it again every seven or eight years," Mao said to the entire country, referring to the Cultural Revolution. Although Mao was no longer around, his spirit has lingered for much longer, even to this day. Everyone was afraid that history might repeat itself, and thus were careful to avoid taking the wrong side or saying the wrong thing, even within their families. As the saying goes, "Once bitten by a snake, you will be terrified by a well rope for the next ten years."

Regardless of what was behind my parents' intentions for me, they let me make all the critical decisions for myself; and in the end, I think that is the best gift to receive from one's parents: the permission to seek your destiny and to live your own life, even if it means failing from time to time, because don't we all learn the most from our failures?

Decades later, my wife and I did the same for our daughter Cintty, who was born and raised in America. She submitted all her college applications by herself without consulting us, and she was admitted into a prestigious veterinary school to pursue the only career she had ever wanted.

It seemed Cintty had drawn her own roadmap early on and followed it every step of the way. This particularly pleased her each time we mentioned it to our friends, and it made her mom and me equally proud of her.

But when I was her age, I did not have this fire, this drive, within me. Or so I thought. It reminds me of a story my father once told me. For thousands of years, those who wanted to become government officials in China had to pass the imperial examinations. All such test-takers had to author high-quality articles to pass and become government officials for life. Some legendary stories, passed down through generations, suggested that someone who did the best in his writings could become a son-in-law of the emperor.

One aspiring young man worked day and night, working on articles for the examination, but he could not come up with anything. "It seems so much harder for you to write something than for me to give birth to our son," his wife griped one day.

"You have it in your belly, but I don't," the young husband replied helplessly.

That story has stuck with me. My father was a playwright before he took on the leadership position for Shenyang Opera Group, but he only published one play. I sometimes wonder if this story explains why my father gave up writing early in his career. Nevertheless, he seemed to have some faith in me.

When I was in middle school (receiving little actual schooling), my father threw me collections of Chinese classics to memorize—word for word, one chapter a day—which he would test me on in the evenings. As I recall, I could understand very little of those passages, but I gradually grew to appreciate the tones and rhymes as I read them aloud. Over time, I fell in love with those yellow, creased pages.

The four most well-known classic Chinese novels became my favorites (*Journey to the West, Outlaws of the Marsh, Romance of the Three Kingdoms,* and *Dream of the Red Chamber,* all written during the Ming and Qing dynasties). It was partially thanks to my father, but more so because they were the few books allowed, and even encouraged, by Mao during those years. "One has to read the novel *Dream of the Red Chamber* five times before having a say," Mao said, referring to the most celebrated literary masterpiece in Chinese history. I read this 900-page novel cover-to-cover three times.

In TianXi, years later, I could recite many paragraphs from these classics. Breathing in the fresh air of this vast prairie seemed to propel the phrases; they leaped into my mind whenever my eyes fell upon a corresponding scene. The pictures depicted by those words were never more vivid than when they were in front of me. Some parts of the Inner-Mongolian highland would bring this graphic verse into my mind (I have put these sections of prose into English, but only in a free-verse style, as the translation does not allow for the strict poetic meter in the original Chinese):

"Under the hazy sky, in the boundless plains, the breeze lowers the prairie to reveal bovine."

Right before spring began, these words would turn up in my head out of nowhere:

"The warmth of spring water: ducks notice it the first."

When summer neared its end, I would not miss this natural sign:

"One leaf marks the arrival of fall."

And every time I was unpacking something my mom had sent to me, this heart-warming poem from the Tang dynasty, entitled "Wanderlust Son," would rhyme from my lips:

"Mother's sewing thread, wanderlust son's clothing;
Seam it a bit denser, afraid of his belated returning.
Who said a heart, a nurtured blade of grass, meant for nothing?
It is filled with a three-spring blessing."

On many occasions these exact words from hundreds, even thousands of years ago, popped into my head. Thanks to my father's autocratic way, the word pictures from these whimsical classics grew only richer and brighter when I was further along on my life's path. Most of all, it led to me spending joyous hours in solitude, with a book in hand.

"That should be a solid foundation for doing anything that seems tedious, including preparing for GaoKao," my inner voice echoed with some confidence now.

Naturally, liberal arts would be the choice for me, in which GaoKao included five categories: Chinese, mathematics, history, geography, and politics. Looking at these categories, I knew I hardly had any systematic education on—let alone any materials to study—any of them.

"But what else is there to do?" I kept asking myself this same question and never came to a clear answer. Consequently, I asked my mom to send me something I could use to begin my studies from scratch.

Those first three months for preparation slipped by, and our fateful time arrived. Four of us from our Youth Center were going to the exams, which for us were held in the Commune Center middle school. Secretary Cong arranged a horse-drawn wagon to take us there, a most honorary treatment.

During the three days of GaoKao, we lived in student dorm rooms: ten students living on one long huokang. Snow covered the outside world, and it was bitterly cold, but the bed was warm and cozy. Still, several people paced in the snow, books in hand, preparing for their last dash toward the finish line.

Somehow, all I can remember of the test was the huge stove at the center of the room. My eyes were drawn to the flickers of fire in the stove more than to the questions before me. Every minute felt like torture.

The result came a few days later, and I got as far as being notified for a physical exam, just missing that last kick to the college door. Records show that 5.7 million applicants took GaoKao in 1977, and of them, 270,000 people were admitted. That 4.7 percent admission rate was by far the lowest since Mao had taken power in China. I did not make it into that 4.7 percent, which was not a surprise to me, nor, I imagine, would it have been to my parents and siblings.

In March of 1978, those 270,000 educated youths entered colleges. Over the three short months since GaoKao had first been announced, they had transformed their lives from ones of almost complete despair (because one person had closed college doors for eleven years) into lives that were now filled with promise (thanks to another person who had allowed them the chance to study again).

How could so many people (tens of millions, and future generations too) define their successes—or failure—except by praising fate as the single deciding factor in their life's course?

Chapter Twenty

Almost immediately after I missed my first shot at GaoKao, I locked my sights on the next one, which was only a few months away: from July 20 to 22, 1978. Before I left for Shenyang for the Chinese New Year in February of 1978, I told Secretary Cong I wanted to stay in Shenyang this time to prepare for GaoKao. He agreed. I then asked Uncle Zhao to be more attentive to those who stayed in the Youth Center. He was happy to do so.

When I returned to Shenyang this time, it was like riding a time machine back to a place I now hardly recognized. All the political slogans had disappeared, and enthusiasm and good cheer was present on people's faces. Most young people had abandoned their Red Guard status, reflected on their lost youths, and were optimistically exploring their futures. Schools were now open and operating as before. Teachers and intellectuals—rather than workers, peasants, and soldiers—again held their heads high.

On March 18, 1978, the CCP held a National Scientific Conference that was of profound significance to China's modern history. Deng Xiaoping delivered an opening speech and referenced the "Four Modernizations" for the first time, referring to the modernization of agriculture, industry, national defense, and science and technology—all of which could only be achieved after formalizing a robust education system. "The key," he said, "is the modernization of science and technology." Officially, it was what turned the country away from class struggle as the primary path toward modernity.

At the closing ceremony to the National Scientific Conference on March 31, Guo Moruo, then the president of the Chinese Academy of Sciences, delivered a speech entitled "The Spring of Science." It proclaimed the eventual arrival of spring, literally and figuratively.

The statement ended with a poetic sentiment: "This is the spring of revolution; this is the spring of the people; this is the spring of science! Let us open our arms and warmly embrace this spring!"

This speech was broadcast all over the country for days and inscribed in school textbooks for years, for the first time supplanting all political indoctrination. From this moment in modern Chinese history, Deng had set an urgent and daring tone, ushering a nation of one billion people onto a fast-moving train. The whistle had blown, and the train was ready to depart.

Still, my personal world did not seem all that bright and hopeful. For me, it was as if a bitter winter still lingered, unwilling to yield its way to the emerging spring that I was hearing about. Unlike two and half years previously, when I was on my New Long March to TianXi, my heart was no longer racing. I was more like a drifter, with few aspirations for anything beyond my insignificant self.

My parents behaved as if they had just escaped a maze, still wondering how they had ended up trapped within it in the first place. These days, we all spoke less, much less than we had when I was little. The last ten years had taken its toll, upending our family and turning sunny days into endless gloom.

Deep down, my father attributed part of his trouble to my mother's complicated family history. "I could have taken a much higher position in my career, like my college friends, if not for your mom," my father griped to me once.

I could see his point, because I knew several of my father's close friends, all of whom were in more admirable positions. On the other hand, my mom had had a lot to swallow over the years. She never lamented her original decision of giving up all her family's privileges for the cause in which she had once believed, although she received little reward for her sacrifices. I had witnessed firsthand how politics had crushed a country along with generations of its people, including my family.

It could have been worse—much worse—but that did not change the fact of how brutal and ugly radical politics could be. We were all a little dead inside during those ten years; it was akin to a mass-killing, albeit without bloodshed or outright violence.

But what if there would be another Cultural Revolution (by that or another name)? How could we tell evil ideologies from the virtuous ones—assuming such a thing existed—so that we did not have to relearn all the painful lessons the hard way? We were faced with so many ideologies: so many complex political ideas, most simplified down to one word ending in "-ism," such as communism, capitalism, fascism, socialism … the list goes on.

Merriam-Webster defines "-ism" as a noun suffix: 1. A distinctive doctrine, cause, or theory. 2. An oppressive and especially discriminatory attitude or belief.

From this definition, as far as I could tell, this world would most likely be a better place without them.

The question sometimes crosses my mind: why do we find ourselves to be binary, in an either-or situation? Why do we side against each other with one idea or another, an idea that has been boiled down to one simple word that ends in "-ism"?

Why do people often fall for the black-or-white fallacy, when gray is the most common reality?

.

CHAPTER TWENTY-ONE

IN 1978, WHEN DENG took on his position of leadership after Mao's death, he had a favorable atmosphere that was necessary, but not sufficient, to turn China around from social and economic cataclysm. This atmosphere had been developing since 1972, when, in February U.S. President Richard Nixon arrived in Beijing to meet with Mao, the first such visit from a U.S. President since Mao had taken over China. Nixon's historic visit resulted in The Joint Communique of the United States of America and the People's Republic of China, which effectively normalized China-U.S. relations. Then, in the same year, just a month after Yasuo Tanaka was elected Japanese Prime Minister, he followed in President Nixon's footsteps and visited Beijing in September 1972. Sino-Japanese relations were normalized shortly thereafter. As a result, China was no longer a third wheel, a little brother tagging along behind the Soviet Union. Now, it was on a new pathway, one recognized by the Western world.

Internally, Deng aspired to lead the entire country toward the Four Modernizations. Suddenly, America—the number one imperialist in Mao's era—had become the icon for the transformations. All Chinese media turned their focus on the U.S., inciting unprecedented enthusiasm about everything in the Western world, such as flashy dresses, spectacular skylines, stately electronics, and roads teeming with automobiles. Images of America and its people from movies and media reports were all in stark contradiction to what we had previously learned. In Mao's words, it used to be understood that "the working-class people in capitalism live in deep water and dire straits."

Assessing this sudden and exciting shift of Feng Qi, I wondered: Where does it leave me? I wanted to know America and the outside world. But if I ever wanted to be on that path, then English would be another test I would have to pass, and I had never learned a single letter of it. Russian was the designated foreign language I had "learned" on and off, back when China was replicating everything from the Soviet before the early 1970s. At least I had kept some books on that to go back to. Now the U.S. had become the new North Star, replacing that of the Soviet Union. English or not, I wanted to aim where my heart directed me.

This time in Shenyang, from the moment I got up in the morning until midnight, I was either on my bike hopping between classes or at home, my head buried in the five subjects: math, Chinese, history, geography, and politics. I hated math more than anything, but I had to get through it. I had neither time nor the energy for free-thinking; that was not required, anyway. All this was fine with me now that I had a meaningful goal to reach for.

English, though, was an entirely different matter. Fortunately, one of my father's friends had a daughter, Xiao Rong, who was a college English teacher. Our families had been close for many years. Knowing that I aspired to take an English test in GaoKao, she was happy to tutor me twice a week, and after two months, I grew to love it more than any of the other five subjects. But, at the same time, I was most puzzled by it. To build my English vocabulary, I carried a deck of cards full of English words and flipped through them whenever I had more than five minutes of free time.

"Most people complain about the difficulty of remembering English vocabulary," Xiao Rong emphasized during one tutoring session, "but the correct use of prepositions is especially challenging for Chinese students." Her words have resonated in my head ever since, as I struggle with that aspect of the language to this day.

And certain teachings during the Mao era have followed me like a shadow, waiting to present themselves whenever the occasion seemed fitting. While I was learning English, one of Mao's Fundamental Three Stories, which everyone was taught to recite, crept into my head: "Yu Gong Removed the Mountains." The story goes like this: Once upon a time, there was a man called Yu Gong (foolish old man), who had three sons. There were two mountains in front of their house, blocking the way to and from their home. One day, the Foolish Old Man began to dig at the two mountains to remove them, encouraging his sons to join him. "How silly of you to do this! It is impossible for you to dig up two gigantic mountains," said a wise, gray-bearded old man who saw them digging all day long. "When I die, my sons will carry on; and when they die, there will be grandsons, and then great grandsons. Why can't we move them away?" Foolish Old Man replied and went on digging. His sons joined him, then his grandsons, and great-grandsons. Finally, God, who was touched by the spirit of their perseverance, sent two angels to remove the mountains.

Mao had wanted everyone to learn from the Old Fool—or, more precisely, to become the Old Fool—to stop at nothing in trying to reach our goals. The spirit of that Old Fool was what I needed right now: learning five essential subjects, plus English.

However, digging up a mountain and grasping the English language were not the same thing. Yu Gong had sons and grandsons, while I had no one else to rely upon. And I believed that my love of Chinese, especially the Chinese classics, only got in the way; the two languages have little resemblance, but I could not stop trying to compare the two. To put it simply, while Chinese characters, also known as Mandarin, are difficult to memorize and even harder to pronounce for beginners, its grammar rules and sentence structures are rather straightforward since all words have fixed forms, no matter how they're used. For instance, Chinese has no verb tenses (past, present or future), no third-person verb forms, no articles for different nouns, no various possessive forms, no senseless prepositions, and no auxiliary verbs. All these exasperated me then, just as they do now, even after decades living in America. From my point of view, these differences make Mandarin harder to learn initially, but easier to grasp once you grasp its essence. What's more, a person needs only know 1,500 to 2,000 Chinese characters to be fluent; and if you know 2,000-3,000 characters, you can articulate letters and read Chinese newspapers and magazines. Comparatively, the average English speaker needs to know five times as many words to be considered fluent, and those who are university-educated need to know ten times more to proficiently draft articles. So, for those who think Mandarin is more challenging to learn, think again.

I was unfazed, nonetheless. I was back to square one at age twenty. And if I failed this year's GaoKao, there would be the next year, and then the year after that. Mysteriously, the Old Fool was speaking to me now: "You had better get busy digging, young man!"

Chapter Twenty-two

A few weeks after I arrived home to prepare for GaoKao, I learned the hardships of living in Shenyang, now one of the most industrialized cities in China. "We need you to help while your mom and I go to work every day," my father said to me at dinner. "We can't have a housemaid now. No families can." Growing up, we'd always had a live-in maid—that was, until the Cultural Revolution labelled it as 'exploitation.' I did not mind doing chores, but it took time to get used to it.

Growing up in the ideal socialism that Mao had created, there was virtually no inequality present in urban areas. The government set the wages for everyone based on their level of education, seniority, and skills. For instance, the average factory worker made around 35 yuan per month, and government staff made 50 yuan per month (one U.S. dollar was worth less than two Chinese yuan back then). Together, my parents were making over 200 yuan each month, an envious amount by the old standard.

In my memory, our family was always financially well off. At the end of every month, two craft paper envelopes would appear in the right drawer of the living room desk, each containing cash; my parent's monthly salary. Everyone, including our housemaid, my sister, my brother, and later me, just used the money whenever we needed to, whether for family or personal use, such as buying stationery or going to the movies. Our parents never set rules for how to use the money. I admit, I had used some to go out with friends for food and beers during my middle-school years. There was no law for the minimum drinking age then.

Decades later in America, when we had our daughter, Cintty, we allowed her to have a joint credit card with us when she started high school, and she kept it until she had her own family and daughter. My wife and I never set a rule for her in using our money, either. But it worked out well: Cintty was always a responsible spender.

In the old socialist system, before the mid-1980s, the government also provided housing, schools, and healthcare for all urban households. All the necessities, such as food, clothing, and transportation, were inexpensive and under government control. Profiting, by any means, was patently against the Marxist theory; therefore, there was no point in saving money. Life was worry-free—but only if there were adequate supplies in the government-controlled marketplace. And that was a big "IF."

Now that I was in charge of home essentials, I witnessed how limited things were on the store shelves. Most items that were available were on strict rationing—one needed coupons to buy them. Before the Chinese New Year, for example, when every family desired various specialty foods, signs appeared on the windows of food stores as a reminder of the specific rationing rules for the Spring Festival. In China, all marketplaces use Jin for weight; one Jin equals a half-kilogram, or 500 grams. Those signs spelled out the rationing in an extensive list:

Fish: one Jin per person
Egg: three Jin per family
Chicken: one Jin per person
Beef: Hui people (Chinese Muslims) three Jin per person
Pork: three Jin per person
Tofu: 28 pieces per person
Green onion: two Jin per family
Sugar: three Jin per family
Tobacco: 25 packs per family
Baijiu (Chinese white liquor): one bottle per family
Peanuts: 0.6 Jin per person

The list went on and on, covering all the essentials, and people needed to purchase them within ten days of the annual New Year's festival. For the rest of the months, there was a limit of only 0.3 Jin of pork per person, 0.3 Jin of soybean oil per person, and one Jin of eggs per family, per month. In Northeastern China, our provincial leader, whose last name was Chen, earned the nickname "Chen SanLiang," which literally means "0.3-Jin Chen." He was known throughout the country for having such a stringent rationing rule.

In those days, chicken, pork, and eggs were less than one yuan per Jin, which was affordable to most families, but money could not buy them as one wished. Families were limited to things like three Jin of rice and wheat flours per month, while the rest were corn or sorghum. Black markets were viewed as capitalistic, and were not only discouraged but closed by force and without notice.

Still, I found it amazing how a planned economy for a country as big as China could arrange everything for its urban citizens. I never heard of people starving to death during the years I grew up. But that system missed one major piece of the puzzle—supply. Somehow, no planned economy, China's included, could figure out a way to plan their supply well enough to meet the demand. Otherwise, it would have been the best economic model—and the happiest society—on the face of the earth: the closest thing to utopia, a classless nation where people were equal, and everything was plentiful enough to satisfy everyone's needs. I wondered, could this ideal ever be achieved?

The reality, however, was far from rosy. So, rather than limiting our diet to cabbage and potatoes day after day, I needed to look for other foods that were not rationed. Occasionally, I spotted fish being sold just before it would become malodorous, or eggs beyond their expiration date; such moments brightened my day. And if a neighbor found something intriguing in the market, people from the apartment building would flock to the store and stand in a long line to buy it.

Sometimes I missed TianXi for its ample food supply, partly owing to Secretary Cong's special care for us. When a horse or a cow was injured, the meat would go to our Youth Center first. Eggs were inexpensive from the locals, and vegetables went straight from the garden to the table; even the grains in TianXi tasted better than in Shenyang, where they usually stayed in storage for years before hitting the market.

Finally, the collective socialistic structure crumbled along with the Cultural Revolution as supply shortages became more severe in the cities. Facing that tiresome reality, I deemed college to be the only tunnel that could eventually lead me into the light.

As family chores consumed much of my day, I spent extra hours at night in rote memorization of all the materials needed to pass GaoKao without ever really paying attention to the essential meanings. It was as if I were trying to fatten a pig for one last month before the slaughter; but this time, I was the sad pig.

CHAPTER TWENTY-THREE

THE NEXT THREE MONTHS flew by, and the fate-deciding moment, for me and for millions of others, was nearly upon us. I had to go back to TianXi to take GaoKao, as dictated by my Hukou (a household registration system that regulated where everyone in the country officially belonged). I left Shenyang one week before the exam date.

It was a bright summer day in Northern China. I took the same train as I had three years ago, but noticeably absent this time was the deafening roar of the cheering crowds, gongs, and drums. This same educated youth had morphed into a calmer person.

One thousand days of tending the earth, with my back facing the sun and eyes staring at the yellow soil, had been more an inner journey for me than a physical one. It was as if I had gone on a quest with a special yearning, dauntless persistence, and fierce determination, and then discovered there had been nothing there to begin with.

"No, it is not entirely nothing," my inner voice was quick to refute, providing countless images to back up my assessment. What about our host family's genial nature and bonhomie, and Uncle Zhao's calm insight and ingenuity, and Secretary Cong's straightforwardness? Where could I have met such people, as well as the many amiable villagers, anywhere else in the world? During my time in Tian Xi I had come to know myself; and if "knowing yourself is the beginning of all wisdom," as said Aristotle, then these three years would become some of the most treasured times of my life.

What if I could process this part of my experience later and somehow transition through it? Perhaps those early lessons, in conjunction with learning and experiences yet to come, might enable me to become someone more than the person I was now: someone more versatile, someone who enjoyed the simple pleasures, and someone who was broad-minded and fun?

Only if I could first climb out of this rut…

The day before GaoKao, three of us from our Youth Center took the horse-drawn carriage to the Commune Center, again staying in the student dormitory of the middle school. They gave each of us a brick as a pillow, which was suitable for the sultry summer, we were told. The daytime was warm, but it gave way to cool and breezy nights. It was a perfect time to go out by myself, pacing in the woods, and going through my English cards one last time.

Each applicant was allowed to indicate his five preferred majors in any college or university. My first preference for a major was International Trade at the Liaoning Finance and Economic Institute in Dalian City (later, it was renamed as Northeastern Finance and Economic University; the campus is now five times larger than it was in my day). I felt much more focused this time. But there were millions of others out there playing the same game, plus the fresh, high-school graduates who had learned English and all the other subjects in their formal classrooms after the Cultural Revolution had ended. My odds were slim. But the Old Fool's spirit seemed to be on my side.

During the actual exams there was no time for hesitation, suspicion, or fear—no time to even think or assess. Divide and conquer was my only strategy. Before I knew it, the exams were complete. We took the horse-drawn carriage back to the Youth Center. I had no notion of how I'd performed—only relief.

At the end of this grueling journey was our familiar Youth Center—once a hub of activity, full of good cheer and laughter, or sometimes tears and sorrow—but now just two strangely forlorn buildings at the north end of the village surrounded by knee-high weeds. It was now eerily quiet and empty. And so was my heart. This was truly the end of an era, and the conclusion of my New Long March. Nevertheless, the indoctrination of my upbringing continued to haunt me.

"To see if a youth is revolutionary, what is the standard?" Mao once famously said. "If he is willing to join workers and peasants, then he is revolutionary. Otherwise, he is not revolutionary; in other words, counter-revolutionary." Mao had come from peasant stock, and he had relied on millions of peasants to successfully utilize his strategy of 'countryside surrounding the cities and armed forces seizing power' to take over China.

History, however, has repeatedly proven that seizing power is one thing; setting a country on track afterward to achieve sustained growth is entirely another. When Mao became history, Deng turned China around by emphasizing the "Four Modernizations" in place of "mud-leg spirit," literally putting Mao and his political views on the shelf for good—but never as a pariah.

Similarly, I consigned my three-year memory of TianXi to a distant but special and everlasting place in my heart: Mao's philosophy was now consigned to history, but my experiences during the Cultural Revolution remained my own, valued and cherished for what they had contributed to my character.

CHAPTER TWENTY-FOUR

WHILE WAITING FOR THE results of the GaoKao in TianXi, we received an official notification that all the youths who had been sent to the countryside were to return to their original cities. Practically overnight, sixteen million educated youths followed the governmental whip-hand, being herded back and forth. It meant all of us in the Youth Center could move back to Shenyang.

We counted down the days for the trucks to come one last time to pick us up and leave this cocoon for good. The Youth Center became a happy beehive, with everyone hurrying in and out to get one more thing done before departure. In retrospect, I was not sure how I felt—neither thrill nor sorrow, but a combination of mixed feelings.

The first thing that came to my mind was, "What is waiting for me in Shenyang?" Being a factory worker had never appealed to me, but what other choice would I have? I did not dare to imagine that my college dream would come true. In my subconscious mind, I tried to forget the recent GaoKao, superstitiously believing the opposite of whatever I wished for would occur.

A week later three trucks from Shenyang roared into the village to yank us out, as if we were wisdom teeth that did not belong in the mouth of TianXi alongside its other people. Most of the urban youths were cheerful about this turn of fate, racing to move their belongings to the trucks.

That evening I went out to see Secretary Cong, Uncle Zhao, my host-families, Director Tao, and Ma Lin to say my last goodbyes. Our firm handshakes said more than words could express. For there was nothing to say—nothing that could make sense for them as well as for me—because we were all just chess pieces being selectively moved on a massive chessboard.

The next day everyone from our youth center, including Uncle Zhao (as our local representative), took several horse-drawn wagons to the nearest county, a trip that took two hours, for our first and the last photo together. I have now forgotten why Secretary Cong did not join us for our only group photo. I think it was because he felt he had already done what he could for us.

In the eyes of the locals, we were undoubtedly the most fortunate people they had known, seen as belonging to the colossal city of Shenyang according to the Hukou system. We consumed all the foodstuffs they produced, those who were born in—and therefore chained to—the secluded hamlet, and they received almost nothing in return. However, everyone had long accepted their lot, as they had many other things that had been around for thousands of years in this middle kingdom.

Reflecting on the re-education experience—our time in TianXi and tens of millions of others elsewhere—many lamented those devastating and wasteful years. Therefore, 'Scar literature' was born as a distinctive genre to commemorate the lives of the educated youths over an anomalous decade of time. Be that as it may, I prefer to remember those years as a vital phase in the alchemy of my personality.

CHAPTER TWENTY-FIVE

WHEN DENG TOOK HIS leadership role in China, I sensed the drastic shift of Feng Qi. The way I saw it, this ancient nation may have finally come to the end of a thousand-year cycle because Deng was so different. For whatever reason, Deng was never Mao's ideal successor; therefore, he was not appointed by Mao upon his last breath. In fact, Deng never held the highest political position in China (the General Secretary of the CCP). Despite that, he had the rare quality to lead China at its most critical crossroad.

And yet, many wonder what made Deng so different from Mao? After all, they fought side-by-side throughout their adult lives, defending the same ideology; how could their worldviews be so different in their later years?

Mao was known to have absorbed his insights and passions from traditional Chinese history; he was, to a great extent, a continuation of the dynastic cycles that had perpetuated for thousands of years in China.

While Mao immersed himself in the Chinese classics, its feudal system, and the essence of all the royal power struggles, Deng, among many other idealistic youths, went to France in early 1920 on a work-study scheme when he was sixteen, where he became acquainted with Marxism and was inspired by the far more industrialized societies in Europe.

While sweating in the factories alongside French workers, Deng understood the working-class people and recognized the importance of uniting them as the primary means of overthrowing Chiang Kai-shek's corrupt government in China. Furthermore, he had witnessed what the French Revolution had done to free its economy by eradicating the constraints of feudalism. He understood that promoting education and technology was the only way to transform a society from feudalism to modernity.

Now, with Mao out of his way and China at its most critical moment, it was time for Deng to usher China into the direction he had envisioned. In doing so, however, there was no one before him he could follow: no playbook ever written, no lucid doctrine ever created. Therefore, no one could tell what would happen in the years to come.

I took the current Feng Qi as a favorable omen, and told myself, "I don't want to miss out on it—whatever the future might hold."

While anxiously waiting for the dust to settle in Shenyang, the official results of the 1978 GaoKao finally came out. This time, out of 6.1 million people taking the countrywide examinations, 402,000 students had passed the required scores, making the admission rate 6.6 percent. This two percent higher admission rate from the GaoKao that had failed me on my first attempt turned my wishful thinking into something more hopeful.

An official letter arrived the next day. My heart pounded, and my hand would not stop trembling. But it only turned out to be a notification for me to report to Shenyang Electric Fan Factory for work, together with a few of my TianXi comrades. Once again, we were being herded into unknown territory. Most of us, in fact, were all waiting for it, since we were all accustomed to being spoon-fed by the government as our only means of survival.

During those years only the fortunate received factory jobs due to the rigid central-planning system. Most other sent-down youths, even after returning to the cities, still lived like outcasts, because the shoddy economy could not absorb so many people at once. It was also because people of our generation had neither education nor skills. Ours was a generation largely written off by society, except for the small percentage who passed the high standard needed to reach the threshold of college doors.

We had long accepted this way of life: to allow the government to arrange all essential matters for us. "People don't loathe poverty, but inequality; they don't despise scarcity but instability", Confucius stated, summing up the mindset of our culture.

Could Confucius's words still hold true in the twenty-first century? Does that explain why, despite everyone amassing far more wealth than ever before, few seem happier?

Either way, I could not see myself riding a bike to work every day as an apprentice, with a canteen lunch box under my arm, counting my fifteen-yuan salary at the end of each month. Therefore, GaoKao was, by far, the one thing on my mind.

In fact, the entire country watched it, as a deep-rooted tradition. In old-time China, even in a small, remote village, if one young man scored a success in the Emperor State Examination, then it became the only story in that village for days, if not months. It was as if a chicken had suddenly burst into flames to rise as a phoenix overnight. This same old sensation was resurrected as colleges finally reopened after eleven years.

And yet, we all had to report to the factory before my wish could be granted. We then had one week of free time before starting work.

"So-and-so was admitted into college." Word on the street spread. At the dinner table that evening, I mentioned it to my parents. My mom said she would call someone she knew, who was a high-ranking officer in Chifeng City. He would have access to all the test results in that area, including TianXi. I hadn't known my mom was so eager to find out if I had gotten in, because she had never shown it before now.

No one had phones in their homes, so my mom went to work the next morning much earlier than usual to make the call. Before I was ready for breakfast, she returned. Her face was infused with joy, and her eyes glowed in a way I had never seen before. She told me the wondrous news: I had been admitted to my preferred college, and for my chosen major.

I remember holding my mom's hand while jumping up and down like a little boy. My father was about to leave for work. His face beamed with delight while he tried to maintain his usual appearance, as if he had already seen it coming.

Immediately, a massive load was lifted from my chest. The Old Fool was not illusory after all. Even pigs could fly, if they tried hard enough. I started to believe miracles did exist, but only for those who set their hearts and minds on something. This moment was the biggest turning point in my life. It released a bird within me, a bird that had suddenly realized the sky was its only limit.

CHAPTER TWENTY-SIX

"*GŌNGXĬ!*" "*GŌNGXĬ.*" (CONGRATULATIONS!) BECAME the greeting by which everyone met my father, my mom, and even my sister and brother the day after my admission letter arrived. All of our faces held smiles, but most especially mine—I was headed to college!

The apartment building where we lived in Shenyang, nicknamed "5.7 building," was constructed for returnees who had followed Mao's instruction to take the "5.7 Road" by going to the countryside. When people like my parents returned, the government constructed many cookie-cutter style apartment buildings to meet the demand. Several of them lined the street, all six-stories in height with red bricks. Several families shared the same entry and hallway. We lived on the second floor, with the Yang family as one of our next-door neighbors. Our two families had always been close, because our parents had known each other long before moving into the building.

The Yang family had a daughter, Xiao Jun, who was six years younger than me, so she called me WangCheng Ge (big brother). She was in middle school. Her father (I called him Yang Bobo, meaning "big uncle," because he was older than my father) was the Labor Bureau Chief of the Shenyang municipal government: a high-ranking official in the city. He was the one who arranged work for people like me, and before my admission letter arrived, offered to get me into a factory I liked.

Xiao Jun's mom was a charming secretary who worked in the same Labor Bureau as her husband, fifteen years her senior. Xiao Jun was the only child in this loving family, and was obviously pampered. From time to time, we would run into each other in the hallway; we hardly said more than a few words. She giggled more often than she spoke, but she always looked directly into other people's eyes.

After Xiao Jun learned that I had been admitted into college, majoring in foreign trade theory and practice, she knocked on our door the next day. "Can you teach me English, WangCheng Ge?" she said to me, as if she merely needed to borrow a pencil sharpener.

At first, I thought it was a joke. "I've only practiced English for three months," I said with a smile. "I'm not very good."

"But you are already admitted to college to learn foreign things, so you must be good…" She fixed her eyes on me, the method she likely used to get what she wanted within her family.

"Okay, we can try, but don't laugh at me." I had a few weeks before college started, and in the end, I agreed as a gratitude to her parents, who were always genuinely nice to me.

Xiao Jun's mom was pleased with the idea, sending us a fruit basket even before we started. Three times each week after breakfast, I would hear a knock at the door. Xiao Jun appeared outside and would ask me to come to her room, usually by tilting her head with her pure, limpid eyes.

The English lessons went smoothly, since her middle school English textbook was far too simple. I brought the stack of cards I had made for myself so that we could start the way I had begun (I had never had an English textbook). A week later, however, I noticed Xiao Jun was not paying attention or following anything I said. Instead, she looked down, staring at a pink diary. When I looked at the book, it was full of her handwriting, but of the same two words: Wang Cheng. It puzzled me. "What's the matter, Xiao Jun?" I asked.

Xiao Jun did not say a word, uncharacteristically timid and unsure of herself. Then she murmured through her teeth, "Can we be friends?"

In those years, friends between a girl and a boy carried a special meaning, especially the way she'd said it, and I realized that this situation was anything but ordinary. She had always been a little sister to me, and therefore her question caught me more than a little off guard.

I played for time to search for something to say. "You are too young to understand what it even means," I stuttered. To be honest, I did not understand it myself, because I had never had a girl I could refer to as a "friend."

There was a lengthy pause, as if we were competing to see who could hold their breath the longest. While Xiao Jun faced down, it allowed me to have a closeup look at someone in a way I never had before, let alone an exquisite and innocent girl. I studied her delicate features, which I had never noticed. Her shining hair was neatly grooved and parted to both sides, with just a curled thread dangling down her face. Two natural, permanent dimples were sculpted into her cheeks as a result of her habitual giggling. But her usual giggles had disappeared today.

I tenderly explained, "I will be far away at college for four years—" I was cut off before I could finish my thought.

"I can practice being a friend while you are away, just like you want me to practice English." She gazed up again, looking hopeful, as if she had found a way out of a maze.

Before I said anything, she got out of her chair and walked to a flowerpot. She picked a camellia stem with about a dozen leaves, holding it out in front of me. Ignoring the flower, she started at the top of the stem and began picking leaves one at a time as she spoke: "You like me, you like me not, you like me, you like me not..."

Before she reached the end, I stopped her.

"As sweet as you are, I'm sure many handsome boys will want to be your friend." I appeared to be back to my senses now, finding a practical way to untangle this knot. "My college is in Dalian, eight hours by train from here. And I don't think I will return even after college." I finally finished a complete chain of thought and took a breath in relief.

It was true, though: my mind was already set on somewhere else, and I was uncertain how far it would go, or what I would settle on in the years to come.

"Besides, you are an only child," I pointed out. "Your parents will never let you out of their sight, even for a day."

By now, Xiao Jun had lowered her eyes without a word. Before I knew what to think next, she stood up, turned around briskly, and ran to the next room, slamming the door behind her. After that day, we did not share eye contact.

Two years later, when I ran into Xiao Jun again during a college break, she told me that her parents did not like the idea of her going to college because she would leave Shenyang and might never return. Her father had arranged a terrific civil position in the government for her, plus a comfortable apartment for her family.

"What is it like living at college, Wang Cheng Ge?" she asked me, looking far more mature than she had two years before.

Seeking a simple way to describe it to Xiao Jun, I said, "College is like ... the biggest restaurant, with an all-you-can-eat menu that everyone can choose from, as much as you can handle—a fun place if you know what you want." I had never thought about college in terms of this metaphor before. "But there are other ways to get what you want, since China is full of opportunities for everyone now," I added, thinking about what she had said about college not being what her parents wanted for her.

Six more years passed before I met her again, living with her parents and working for the municipal government in Shenyang, just as her father had planned for her. After a few rounds of arranged dates by her parents' friends, she was married to a handsome young man, a retired soldier who worked in the city's HR department. In fact, my mom told me that she had introduced the boy to Xiao Jun since our two families had remained close. I felt happy for her when my mom told me about Xiao Jun's marriage.

Another two decades later, I met Xiao Jun and her husband when they came to see my mom. Their daughter had just finished college (all the urban high-school graduates went to college by that time). With the help of her father, Xiao Jun had arranged for her daughter to work in the Shenyang government. They were trying to match Xiao Jun's daughter with the right young man so that they could all work and live near one another.

My mom told me that Xiao Jun and her husband came to see her every year right before the Spring Festival, and they always brought a basket of New Year's presents, such as a bottle of cooking oil, a bag of fine grain, a bottle of baijiu, and a duck or a chicken to represent goodwill. I could tell that Xiao Jun was content.

"If there is an ordinary but happy life," I thought to myself years later, "Xiao Jun's life is an example of it."

As for myself, I have traveled halfway around the world, constantly seeking a fulfilling way of life; however, millions of people like Xiao Jun (including most of my middle school, college, and TianXi friends) seem to have found it right where they were born and raised.

Some people compare life to a journey, but do they mean it to be an extended guided-tour with a planned start, a foreseeable end, and most events already arranged? Or can it be a less-traveled road that encounters and embraces the unexpected along the way? I guess it all depends on one's insatiable curiosity as opposed to his need for security. There is no right way or wrong way; only the way of each individual.

CHAPTER TWENTY-SEVEN

I HAD EXPECTED MY college life to include toiling into the wee hours to retain mountains of knowledge and prepare for weekly exams—but it was not so.

Later, I learned that I was admitted into the Foreign Trade Department mostly due to my other skills rather than my overall test scores, the least of which was my English test, in which I scored a measly 26 out of 100 points. I could barely write one complete English sentence without an error. And my math score was only 20 points, part of which must have been lucky guesses as I stumbled through the multiple-choice questions.

After we passed the minimum total scores in GaoKao, our department heads considered our overall qualities, which they valued more than the test results. It was a rare but shrewd policy, because they saw people with comprehensive capabilities instead of special analytical skills as a better fit to work in the field of international commerce.

Consequently, my past as a Production Unit Captain and Youth Center lead in TianXi helped me to gain admittance. I was also a good ping pong player. Back when we lived in Daqing, I represented our Commune in a city-wide tournament competing against all middle school kids. My performance in TianXi and my musical talents (as illustrated by passing my audition for the Shenyang Conservatory of Music) carried weight in my favor. Past experiences and demonstrable aptitudes apparently made up for my definite lack of English and math competence.

Regardless of how we'd each gotten into college, the rest was entirely up to us. I felt the Foreign Trade major was an odd one after I got to know it better. We did not have Chinese literature or history; also, there was no math or statistics. Western economics and finance were marginalized, because Marxist Political Economics was still the mainstream back then. English became the only subject that required our full attention—that, and limited international trade practices and case studies left us with plenty of free time.

I had always enjoyed reading as a pastime, and one book I found particularly thought-provoking was *Economics* by Paul Samuelson, the first Western economics text originally written in English that I read. His prose was exceedingly engaging, and the theory was easy to understand. However, I could not stop comparing this new perspective to Marxist theory.

According to Marxist political and economic theory, profit comes from exploiting the working class; therefore, capitalists were synonymous with parasites, living on the backs of workers. Capitalists attempted to extract as much surplus value as possible, and another name for profit was "exploitation rate."

"If money," according to Augier, "comes into the world with a congenital bloodstain on one cheek, then capital comes dripping from head to toe, from every pore, with blood and dirt."—Karl Marx, in *Capital, Vol. 1: A Critical Analysis of Capitalist Production*.

Even a few decades later, in 2019, when the South Korean hit movie *Parasite* became the most-talked-about dark horse in Hollywood and beyond, my college friends in China debated who the "parasites" were that the movie referred to in this tug-of-war between rich and poor. Was it the super-rich family living in the fancy castle, or the humble bunch providing services to the wealthy?

How could I reconcile these two world views? Was there a clear-cut response to settle any social debates satisfactorily for all sides?

All name-calling aside, Marxist political economics taught us that the effort to extricate profit from workers, followed by resistance from said workers, was the primary cause of class warfare. All of this would, someday, lead to a revolution by the workers to take over the capitalist world.

Interestingly—and rather deliberately—that was how the movie *Parasite* ended: in a bloody class warfare.

However, in *Economics* by Paul Samuelson, maximizing profit was the core of capitalism and the ultimate drive of all economic behavior in modern society. It was—and still is—motivated by self-interest as human nature. Therefore, profit, the way I understood it, greased the wheels of the economy, a powerful but invisible hand driving any advanced and thriving civilization.

The two viewpoints toward 'profit' could not be more contradictory, and there seemed to be no way that both could be true.

"Who are the capitalists, anyway?" I shouted inwardly. "Are they a different species from the rest of us?"

But from all the American movies, there were neither two distinct types of people, nor any signs of exploitation. Besides, Mao had followed Marxism to take over China, and then gotten rid of all the capitalists and landlords. So why did class struggles become even more prevalent throughout the Mao era? My list of questions only grew longer, and I vowed to get to the root of it one day. At least, that was how I saw it at the time.

Later, in America, I found that people made friends with one another even though their home countries were at odds—or even at war. I made friends with people from Taiwan when it was still at war with Mainland China (in 1991, Taiwan proclaimed its war with the People's Republic of China over), and some from Vietnam, India, South Korea, and, most of all, Americans.

Nowadays I wonder why governments cannot get along with one another, even though their people can. Which begs the question: for what, and most of all, for whom do they fight?

CHAPTER TWENTY-EIGHT

In COLLEGE, I was totally naive and often beyond awkward. As a result, I had two or three close friends and wanted almost nothing to do with the rest. That could have explained why I never had a spark with a girl up to that point. But I believe culture played a larger role in shaping my individuality.

Throughout Chinese history, boys and girls were not supposed to make direct contact. "No direct interaction is the only proper etiquette between men and women," according to Mencius (372-289 BC), the most well-known Confucian philosopher. As a tradition, matchmakers arranged marriages until the late 1970s.

In the early 1960s, when I was four, my aunt (who was five years older than my father) lived in a remote and impoverished village in Hebei Province, 600 miles southwest of Shenyang. She had six children, all girls. Her husband died shortly after the last child was born.

My aunt often came to stay with our family for a month or two. Every one of her six daughters would come with her to help with our household chores. More importantly, by staying with us they could all have enough food to eat, which was almost impossible to manage for a single, crippled woman raising six daughters in a poverty-stricken village.

The most striking image I have of my aunt was—and still is—the way she waddled: like a penguin, only slower. She clung to anything her hand could reach when she walked, such as a chair, a table, or just the bare wall. Then I noticed her shoes, which looked like small paper boats, less than four inches in size with a point in the front. No one talked about how it had happened, because it was common for women to be like that in those days.

I later learned this was a deep-rooted Chinese tradition. Starting from the Song Dynasty (960-1279 AD), the wicked custom of foot binding was best known as "three-inch lotus." When a girl was five or six years old, a woman in her family, usually her grandmother, would use long wrapping clothes to bind her little feet all day, everyday, into that shape and size. Like how a boxer tightly wraps his fists before entering the ring; only for those girls, the wrapping cloths were on their feet their entire lives—something they could not take off if they wanted to walk later in life.

The purpose of the custom was to please men in an idiosyncratic and erotic way. At first, only the girls who were selected to serve in the palace would bind their feet. Over time, the idea spread to upper-class citizens, then to ordinary people—if they wanted to see their daughters married into wealthier families. Over a thousand years, this practice slowly became the norm for Chinese women before Mao took over China. I could not imagine how my aunt felt, as it was unbearable to see it then—even to think of it now.

One might wonder what such tiny-footed women could do, other than being restricted to a space no larger than a bedroom or a kitchen. And that was precisely the point. Serving men's needs and doing the household chores were all that men—and society—expected women to do. As time went by, that became the standard of style that elegant women chose to follow.

Fortunately, my aunt did not force her six daughters to bind their feet. In fact, my aunt's generation was the end of this long and humiliating chapter for Chinese women—the Feng Qi had suddenly reversed. "Women hold half the sky," Mao said. He denounced this regressive and cruel practice and encouraged all women to play an equal role with men at work and at home—and in schools.

By the time I was in middle school in the early 1970s, girls and boys were assigned to sit side-by-side. During those years, boys and girls viewed each other entirely as equals—an idea instilled in our young heads by Mao. But even then we hardly ever made eye contact, let alone had a conversation. And no girl or boy would express fondness towards one another; we did not know how. In retrospect, it was not a typical scene even in the animal kingdom.

Now, entering college in the late 1970s, Feng Qi among our forty-eight college classmates had shifted yet again and turned into anything but traditional. Classmates sat in the same classroom every day, and we lived in the same building for four years, with eight bunk beds in each dorm. Even so, 'dating' was never a word in our vocabulary, although we were all thinking about it, as all boys and girls do. And yet, girls always knew how to get things started.

The girls in our class were not only more mature, but also intelligent enough to take control of this delicate process. They often started it by asking just the right boy to be an English dialogue partner, while gradually strengthening their relationship down the road. Overall, because of the comparative forwardness of these tactics, nearly all the girls found their dialogue partners before the end of the first year in college. And right after graduation, seven couples had formed out of our class of forty-eight—only eleven of whom were girls. The transformation of women's roles has continued into the twenty-first century, paralleling the dramatic changes in China as a whole. Some changes happened before the world's eyes, like skyscrapers rising out of the paddy terraces all over the country. Others were fast evolving but indiscernible, like the progression of Chinese women. "Millennials" became a trending word in the media, and a recognizable force in the U.S. and China. Society regarded them as a generation utterly different from their parents, a phenomenon especially more pronounced for the Chinese.

The 'one-child policy' officially written into the Chinese constitution in 1978 remained in effect until 2016. That made all the millennials the only child in their families. And then, the rapid economic development fostered ever-increasing socioeconomic inequality as an unwanted byproduct of prosperity. Furthermore, the open-door policy allowed Chinese people to taste Western culture for the first time in history. American pop culture and individuality—symbolized by Rambo, Michael Jackson, and Madonna, among others—was like adding fuel to the fire. It sped up the changes in how Chinese millennials viewed the world and themselves. These dynamics entirely re-wrote the chapter about Chinese women, a theme unrecognizable by the older generations, including mine.

It used to be that women's bodies were their means for survival, even at the cost of mutilation. Now, they were breaking free and setting standards for what they wanted for themselves. More specifically, as wealth became the determining factor in relationships, women wanted to see a man own an apartment and have a promising career before starting anything serious with him.

Women could get what they wanted, accumulate wealth, maintain enviable careers for themselves, and enjoy life the way they chose. Meanwhile, men had ways to get what they wanted, including easy and inexpensive access to women for a one-night stand. So why bother with marriage? Census figures for China show that around twenty-five percent of women aged twenty-five to twenty-nine choose not to marry, which had been only five percent just two decades prior.

Now that both men and women had faced abrupt changes, both needed constant mental adjustments to make their relationships work. China's divorce rate jumped thirteen percent in 2014 alone, reaching as high as twenty-seven percent in 2015, according to research; whereas the divorce rate had been only two percent in the 1970s and fourteen percent in the 1990s.

By no means am I implying that Chinese women are at fault for driving up the divorce rate; women's gender roles have undergone the most revolutionary changes, but there are many other factors. Nevertheless, women deserve equal education and should pursue what they want—just as much as men do.

Then again, millennials are young yet, and their attitudes towards each other—and toward life in general—are still evolving. "Hope rests upon all of you [youths]." And Mao's wish will be fulfilled over time.

CHAPTER TWENTY-NINE

THE DAWN OF ECONOMIC revival broke in 1978, which was also the year I entered college. Then again, "Economy is like an airplane," Paul Samuelson stated in *Economics*, "it either moves forward or comes down." With plenty of free time in college and a more curious mind than ever, I tried to decipher what had been happening within the country. Was everything that had happened during my youth merely a mirage? I wondered. Other than mainstream media, *Voice of America* on the radio became another window into the real China and the world—my legitimate excuse to learn English, if I got caught listening to it.

Although Mao Zedong did not pick him as his successor, as the Vice Premier of the State Council, Deng Xiaoping was already the CCP's de facto leader. But that did not mean Deng could just turn this humongous ship around right away. The strong political undercurrent was a statement commonly referred to as the "Two Whatevers." They were: "We will absolutely uphold whatever policy decisions Chairman Mao made, and unswervingly follow whatever instructions Chairman Mao gave." These appeared as headlines in all the major newspapers across the country, making it feel as if Mao were still in charge.

Being fully aware of the daunting prospect, Deng laid the ground-work to unite the country ideologically by preserving Mao's doctrine. He required the CCP to "completely and accurately understand Mao Zedong's theories." He then glossed over one crucial detail: "We also need to break mental shackles and liberate our thoughts.

"There are two tasks before us," Deng continued. "First, we must connect theory with reality. Second, all propositions need to come from a practical point of view. Currently, people's minds are too rigid, and everything has to come down from the very top." Here, Deng was referring to the mantra of "Two Whatevers." He then emphasized, "'Seeking truth from facts' is the most significant part of Chairman Mao's [doctrine]. Without this spirit, there will be no hope for the Four Modernizations." Without rejecting Mao's ideas in the minds of the people, Deng put this pragmatic stance into practice to rescue China from economic and social calamity.

After Deng had orchestrated the overture, the curtain went up for the main event: The 3rd Plenary Session of the 11th Central Committee of the Communist Party of China, which was held in Beijing from December 18 to December 22, 1978. This pivotal event unleashed a series of epoch-making policies that have affected everyone in China to this day.

This historical turn was reflected in a few areas, starting with a fresh tone being set for all the members of the CCP. They had to face reality and stick to the truth instead of preaching the political propaganda of the past; to liberate thoughts and ideas and uphold the daunting task of economic reform and opening-up.

"Reform and opening-up" had never been mentioned before, let alone proposed as a fundamental economic goal and policy for the entire country to follow. That positioned Deng Xiaoping as the chief architect of the reforms and the mastermind behind the economic engine in China.

To ensure the unambiguity of his idea, Deng said in 1978, "Let some people get rich first, driving through the region, and reaching common prosperity for the country." He could not be any clearer. The session adjourned having instituted specific measures to enforce the policies of economic reform.

In rural areas, the Contract and Responsibility System was introduced as a breakthrough reform: contract farming to each household. Once considered 'pure capitalism' in the Mao era, it became a top economic policy. The policy was adopted by nearly everyone, and quickly spread throughout the country. The contract guaranteed a fair percentage of the harvest was allocated to the local government at a reasonable price, and then the rest would be for the household to keep. The new policy changed the status of peasants from mere laborers in the collective system to co-owners of their land. This solved one deep-rooted problem of egalitarianism in the collective economy that Mao had borrowed from the Soviet Union in the early 1950s.

In urban areas, Deng's reforms expanded the autonomy of for-profit businesses as a prelude to introducing private enterprises to China. Suddenly, as though a whistle were blown, everyone began to run, racing for money. All kinds of stores and vendors suddenly lined the streets: food, clothing, books, electronics, and video tapes. Some of the videos were legal, while others were not, like pornography, which had not existed during Mao's time. But the city regulators knew when to inspect the inventory seriously and when to look the other way, depending on the social and political Feng Qi.

After this milestone conference, the CCP formed a central leadership with Deng Xiaoping at its core (although Hua Guofeng was still the General Secretary of the CCP, and Deng Xiaoping was the Vice Premier of the State Council). The well-documented history of China's miraculous economic growth has been ongoing well into the twenty-first century.

Times changed, and Maoist doctrine officially fell by the wayside; however, it was never discarded altogether. That was the Chinese way: to enthusiastically worship and follow the strong man as they insatiably longed to be led. And Mao was the strongest man in China's modern history, despite his severe faults in his later years. In the mind of the ordinary Chinese, it was Mao who had rescued them from "living in the boiling water and sweltering fire," something similar to Moses leading the Israelites out of Egypt.

Does a nation need a spiritual pillar to unify its people and move forward in unison? Deng seemed to think so. And no one else had been able to fill that role except Mao. Even to this day, since the founding of New China in 1949, Mao's portrait is still displayed on the Watchtower of the Forbidden City in Beijing. More interestingly, in Beijing one can find two long queues daily: one is typically lined with hundreds of people waiting to enter the Chairman Mao Memorial Hall, the sacred hall where Comrade Mao Zedong rests; the other line is for those waiting by the gate of the U.S. Embassy for visa applications.

Some people cannot let go of a past that lives within their hearts, while others heed the voices in their heads that encourage them to build a better future. I think many people hold both views at the same time—reminiscing about the past while looking towards tomorrow. We humans are more complex than just believing one way or another. "Follow your heart but take your brain with you," said Alfred Adler.

CHAPTER THIRTY

College was fun. More particularly, it was a time and place for us to mature rapidly. I felt like I was going through a rebirth: just a year before, I was tending the earth in TianXi. I needed to get to know myself all over again.

During Mao's time, the traditional form of education was to channel young people to become successors of proletariats, such as workers, soldiers, engineers, doctors, and nurses. I believed Mao's intention was noble, despite his limited worldview. But, somehow, none of these images ever appealed to me, even during those years when I aspired to becoming a real proletariat. Now that the radical idea had died, my idealism still remained.

It is easier to alter rivers and mountains than one's nature, an old Chinese saying goes. Obviously, I needed something to fill the void: something to accelerate my inner drive.

For a time, I considered exploring a belief in the supernatural as my guiding star. But somehow, the more I read and thought about it, the less it seemed to click with me (although I adored all the beautiful verses). I was far from alone as a nonbeliever among one billion people in the country. I faulted the culture in which we grew up.

Throughout China's history, movements were manifest for making Confucianism a proper religion. In times long past, Confucius had been a Godlike figure. But as the centuries passed, people regarded Confucianism only as a philosophy: the fundamental principle of ethical discipline. Confucius remains a teacher and a philosopher to this day, decidedly an earthly figure in the eyes and minds of his countrymen, albeit the most influential one in history.

I am reminded of Jesus of Nazareth, whom I learned later in life was a Jew, as were his earliest followers. Many Jews regard him as a Jewish teacher; it was only centuries after his death that Christianity, as a separate religion, emerged. I have to wonder if there is a resemblance between these two outstanding teachers in the eyes of their own people.

According to the Chinese philosopher and historian, Fung Yu-Lan, Confucianism was defined as a "state ethic" starting from the Han Dynasty. Largely because of that influence, Chinese people have a far more pragmatic way of thinking, molded by its tradition thousands of years in the making.

Confucianism emphasized a practical approach to understanding life—not death—for the purpose of serving the emperor (never God). Confucius' teachings were pounded into the people, thus turning this 9,600,000-square-kilometer country into a barren land for any higher beings to take root, even before Mao's time. It was not like there were no such attempts in the past, but none had succeeded somehow. And Mao put one last nail in that coffin.

Throughout my coming-of-age years, Mao reinforced atheistic ideas in his indoctrinations: "Foolish Old Man Moves Mountains" is one typical example. He emphasized that people could—and should—conquer nature. We must believe in our own eyes and our ability more than anything else to handle the circumstances we encounter. And even after Mao's death, the entire country had taken his words into their hearts, although sometimes in ways not intended. After Deng sounded the marching horn of economic reforms, people have wholeheartedly placed their newfound faith of wealth accumulation and mercantilism in the spirit of the Old Fool.

After having renounced my fictional idol of Soviet revolution from the novel *How the Steel Was Tempered*, and after a failed quest for spiritual faith, I still needed something to restore my inner strength. On the first page of a new diary, I wrote a vague goal: *An intellectual mind and an athletic body.* It was like a fresh path with no beginning, no ideals, and no perceived destination. I left all my senses wide open to new ideas.

CHAPTER THIRTY-ONE

IN COLLEGE, WE HAD no elective classes because there was a shortage of teaching staff so soon after reopening universities. Aside from a few hours to study English each day, the rest of my time was for me to squander. But there were plenty of other activities. And most of them fell into the category of my new, solemn pledge, "an intellectual mind and athletic body."

Our college held an annual Track and Field sporting event, which lasted for a full three days. Hurdling appealed to me with its speed, agility, and full-body coordination. After some practice, I could do well enough to earn a second place in this category: two solid points for our class.

Music seemed to be in my genes, at least as a hobbyist. Since I could play several instruments—violin, accordion, Hu Qin (Chinese violin), and bamboo flute—I fit into any music event. But nothing compared to my latest undertaking, which became the heyday of my college years.

When the college art director proposed a play, he picked me to be the male lead. The play was entitled *Son of the Artillery Commander*—a love story tinged with satire on the superficial Feng Qi of society.

In those years, one's family background carried far more influence on young people, including with whom they should—or should not—fall in love. I was electrified during production, as the play somehow fit in with my zeal for an ideal society.

The play was about a girl from an intellectual family. She secretly fell in love with a working-class boy: the role I played. Meanwhile, the girl's parents had a family friend, a high-ranking army commander who also had a son. The girl's father wanted his daughter to befriend the army commander's son, who was also expressing affection for her.

It so happened that the father of this working-class boy oversaw the building of a high factory chimney. People likened the chimney to the long barrel of a cannon; therefore, he got himself the nickname of "artillery commander" from everyone around him. Since the girl was most certain her father would disapprove of her boyfriend being a working-class young man, she introduced her boyfriend as the son of an artillery commander when she brought him to meet her family. Her father was so delighted to meet this young man because of his "elite family status," and so he arranged a lavish feast to receive his future son-in-law.

However, many days later, the father learned that this young man was, in fact, from a simple working-class family. Yet, it was too late and too obvious to reject the boy without losing face. By the end, the father, with an utterly awkward grin, accepted his daughter's relationship with this bright, working-class young man.

We discussed the script and rehearsed the play two hours a day for more than a month. To celebrate the Moon Festival, we performed it on stage in the largest auditorium our college had, and then gave encore performances at other colleges around the city. It was exhilarating to play a part in this apolitical show, and through it to express my ideals for others to see.

The evening after the final curtain call, the girl who played my counterpart in the show came up to me and asked if I could go out with her to the city center during the coming weekend. Our college was on the outskirts of Dalian City. Going to the city for a movie and unusual cuisine was the most enjoyable way to spend the weekend. But I happened to have had plans for that weekend; hence, I nicely told her I could not go. She lowered her eyes, turned around, and walked away. That was the last time I saw her.

Somehow, this scene—her two large, twinkling eyes on her pink-tinged cheeks—stuck in my mind more than all the other scenes with her in the play. Did I say I was a late bloomer? In years past, many 'what-ifs' crossed my mind from time to time, and this was one of them.

Are we emotional creatures, far less rational than we think we are? I believe I am—letting my heart lead the way while my brain tries to catch up. But I only came to this realization in my later years. Even though life does not permit do-overs, I can always go back in my memories, reconstruct my journey, and see past events with new eyes.

CHAPTER THIRTY-TWO

FOUR FUN-FILLED YEARS of my college time elapsed. Toward the end, jobs—those we could only have hoped for in the past—were lined up for us. Since we were the first wave of college graduates after the Cultural Revolution, we could literally pick the city, even the institution or company, for which we wanted to work. We had suddenly become the luckiest young adults that had ever come of age in our country, and only one question occupied our minds: What was waiting for us next? We knew that we could work in Dalian, Shenyang, or Beijing, and choose among dozens of commercial companies and government institutions in which to start our careers.

Since I was involved in many activities, and also had been elected head of our class for a term, I had more interactions with our department leaders than most. "Where would you like to go after college: what city and for what company?" the head of our Department, Secretary Yu, asked me one day, granting me preferential treatment.

I locked my eyes on Beijing without a blink. Most Ministries under the State Council had positions for us, such as the Ministry of Machinery, Aviation, Defense, Electronics, Construction, and Agriculture. "I'd like to work in the Ministry of Electronics Industry in Beijing," I told Secretary Yu. And so I received my first official job.

My position was in the China Electronics Import and Export Corporation under the Ministry of Electronics Industry, overseeing the import and export of electronics for the entire country. That was how a planned economy operated. Electronics, I figured, should be front and center in the future of modernization.

Nine of my classmates were going to work within different Ministries in Beijing. Our jobs came with the most sought-after Beijing Hukou in the country. We instantly became the pride of our families, our college friends, and, most of all, ourselves. The night before leaving college, the nine of us got together one last time to sketch out our exciting lives in the capital city. To celebrate our promising new lives, we leaped up together, pouring beers over one another.

Before I reported for work, the 12th National Congress of CCP was held in Beijing on September 1, 1982. Deng Xiaoping, in his opening speech, proposed "building socialism with Chinese characteristics" as a guiding principle for the entire country.

Deng pointed out: "To achieve our modernization, we must face the reality of China's unique situation. We should pay attention to and learn from foreign experiences. However, we will never succeed by directly copying other countries. We learned many lessons from the past. We should combine the universal truth of Marxism with our concrete reality and take our own approach to build socialism with Chinese characteristics."

Deng's historic speech ended with the most ambitious agenda: "We will build our country into a highly civilized, highly democratic, socialist country." His ideology was tempered with pragmatism. It has set China on a path that has been officially labeled as 'socialism with Chinese characteristics' ever since. However, 'Chinese characteristics' have never been explicitly defined, thus leaving it to anyone's interpretation, which has varied and adapted from time to time.

At the end of this consequential conference, the plenary decided Hu Yaobang was to take over as the General Secretary, and Deng Xiaoping would be the Chairman of the Central Military Commission of the Communist Party of China. "Political regime grows out of the gun barrel," Mao once famously said. It was clear who held the ultimate authority at this time.

However, back then, not even Deng himself had a clear idea of what "socialism with Chinese characteristics" should look like. Many still debate it even four decades later. Deng openly admitted that "he likened his way of economic reform to crossing the river by feeling the stones." Nevertheless, Feng Qi had never included more resoluteness, promise, and hope for this ancient land—as if a sleeping giant were finally awakened before the world's eyes.

Regardless of what the catchphrase "socialism with Chinese

characteristics" was intended to depict, it had filled the entire country with the resolve to get into the race at full speed—this time for our own sakes instead of that of an elusive ideology.

Chapter Thirty-three

Once again I pulled up roots, dragging the two large suitcases that had accompanied me from Shenyang to TianXi, Dalian, and now to Beijing. This time, the train I boarded was destined for the Middle Kingdom's heart. It was a dream job in a dream place.

The China Electric Import and Export Corporation (CEIEC) had its head office in Beijing with branches in most major cities and many foreign countries. In a centralized economy, the Ministry of Electronics had allowed CEIEC absolute power over its branch companies and electronic factories around the country for all import and export businesses. CEIEC decided what electronic products to support and how to compensate those factories.

In 1982, I was the only one in CEIEC who had formal international business and English training. All the other fresh college graduates were from engineering majors. They needed to go through a one-year workshop before they could work. Meanwhile, I was assigned right away to work in the First Export Department, handling the hottest electronic products for export.

I worked independently, starting from the second day after I met everyone in our department. The head of the department, Lao Sun, started his day at the office with a tea thermos in his hand and ended the day with the same tea thermos, with countless refills in between. The only English he could speak was "Sank'u." Consequently, he tossed me a full selection of products from various electronic manufacturers. "Study these products, Xiao Wang, to select the ones that could be sold in America first. And let me know." I was once again being referred to by this name, "Xiao Wang," as I was the youngest in the company.

The rest of the time, as I recall, Lao Sun would talk about tea—

what tea would be best to start off the morning, to have after lunch, and then that last cup in the late afternoon, just when you were inclined to doze off.

I used to think milk tea, from my TianXi years, was the best. Now I learned that there were at least a dozen other kinds of tea, with major categories such as black tea, yellow tea, white tea, green tea, oolong tea, pu'erh tea, and many others named after their originating locations.

"Even a seemingly simple routine can be a wealth of interest and intrigue if you pay close attention to the details," Lao Sun said to me while preparing his first tea of the morning, as if he were talking about how I should do my work. I'd never had any reason, nor the patience, to try different types of tea until now.

The transition from milk tea to all the popular ones was effortless because there was no milk tea outside Inner-Mongolia. Following Lao Sun, I got into a habit of starting my day with a tea mug on my desk for the entire time I worked at CEIEC. "With a tea mug in my hand, I would look more like a seasoned businessman." That was my reasoning for tea at first.

Over time, I grew to realize the deeper meaning of this dependency. Other than its subtle but distinctive aroma and dulcet earthy flavors, the deliberate preparing and supping ritual was close to a state of Zen; I could quiet my inner voice and slow my mind to start the morning. It helped me ease into a fast-paced workday, and sometimes into the late night.

CHAPTER THIRTY-FOUR

DENG REOPENED COLLEGE DOORS to millions, which allowed me to see the country on a much higher plane than I had at any time in the past. In Beijing I witnessed the severe lack of people with proper training in the workplace, even in the highest organizations, such as the country's Electronics Ministry—an intellectual vacuum caused by the devastating Cultural Revolution. To me it showed how politics, shaped by just one man, could annihilate the intellectual and economic fabric of a nation.

For the same reason, this enormous educational chasm made my college background stand out at work. Since no one was able to tell me how I should do my work, I simply experimented along the way. I spent my time either traveling to electronic factories or receiving foreign clients in Beijing. During the weekends, I guided my foreign visitors to see the Great Wall, Forbidden City, Summer Palace, and all the well-known historical sites.

In the evenings, Lao Sun, and sometimes the Senior VP of CEI-EC, would host dinners for our foreign visitors at famous restaurants. I then became an interpreter at the dinner table. Our Senior VP's last name was Zhang, so I called him Zhang Zhong (Zhong being the title for the most senior staff member of a business). He would often show off his Chinese literary talent to his guests, which was also a topic of conversation I enjoyed very much.

Zhang Zhong was directly involved in export, my area of work, and he and I had a similar passion for words. Seeking the proper English terms to carry on an interesting conversation and putting English back into an appropriate, sometimes fascinating Chinese context was often something I wrestled with, but also brought me enormous enjoyment. I often forgot it was a job.

In the eyes of my friends and family, I was living the dream. A fresh college graduates' monthly salary was forty-seven yuan (equivalent to a little over twenty dollars) for the first year, and then fifty-four yuan starting the second year. But working for money was hardly my goal. It was the nature of the work that separated one social status from another that motivated me.

Many electronics factories around the country were eager to sell their products overseas, and I was one of the primary gatekeepers. When I visited these factories, they would treat me like a rock star, to use a modern term, designating a driver to chauffer me everywhere, plying me with the best local food three times a day, and providing snacks 24-7.

Because of the poor-quality state of production, I needed to import critical components and have them assembled in China before exporting the finished products overseas. That was the dawn of China becoming the "World Factory." Entering the twenty-first century, approximately eighty percent of all assembled products in the world took place in China, including iPhones and iPads.

In one particular circumstance, I arranged for one of my clients from Hong Kong to work out a business plan with me in a factory near Wuhan. Usually, foreign visitors came and left, interacting only for a day or two during the business conference. But this time, he and I spent a full one week in Wuhan because of the business' complex nature, which granted me close contact with someone from outside China for the first time.

His last name was Qi. He was around thirty, slim, and of medium height. His neat, but much longer, hair resembled Bruce Lee's. He had small, bright eyes on a delicate face. Even the sunglasses he wore were like a shining label that separated him from the Mainland Chinese. I tried to dress well at work, but it wasn't anything fashionable because of my meager fifty-four-yuan-a-month salary.

Even more interestingly, a secretary accompanied Mr. Qi to Wuhan: a twenty-six-year-old woman, wearing curly hair and flashy clothes like a movie star. They shared one hotel room.

Hong Kong, in those days, was the first window for us Mainlanders to peek out at the Western world and the kind of life Chinese people aspired to.

Mr. Qi and I got along well beyond the business-client relationship. He owned an electronics factory in Hong Kong with 200 workers. During those years, when Mainland Chinese were looked upon as inferior in Hong Kongers' eyes, his candidness made me feel confident about myself. But our interactions outside of our business engagements were more intriguing to me.

"There are three kinds of people in Hong Kong, and they each have different attitudes towards Mainland Chinese," he said. "You can sense it the first minute you meet them. There are those who introduce themselves as 'Hong Kongers, not Chinese' or as 'Hong Kongers' or 'I'm from Hong Kong, China.' And then, you can decide how to mingle without offending them while still getting your work done."

"Many people in Hong Kong believe themselves to be superior to Mainland Chinese; therefore, they do not want to be regarded as Chinese, which is almost synonymous with being uncivilized in their view," he said. "But I see the huge potential in the Mainland people. They are the most driven, focused, and talented people I have known." He followed the chain of thought. "Given the right government policy, China will catch up to, and even surpass, many countries sooner than people think." His candor bonded us closer than any ordinary business relationship.

"I want to go to America to study," I said, as though it was my turn to share my thoughts with him. "I want to know more about the rest of the world." The idea had been in me for years. But I had never mentioned it to anyone until now, let alone to a person from outside China. "Although I've had good luck with my career, I'm not ready to settle in just yet." It was a deep and somewhat risky thought to share with someone I had known for less than a week.

Mr. Qi did not appear surprised, though. "America is a great country, maybe the best for newcomers," he said. "Let me know if you need U.S. dollars for such a major move." Mr. Qi surprised me with his quick and generous offer.

For someone making the equivalent of twenty dollars a month in 1983, buying a plane ticket to the U.S. was no less ambitious than landing on the moon. I would never forget Mr. Qi's gracious gesture, even though I did not take him up on the offer. To me, it would have felt wrong to receive such substantial help on a personal matter from a business client.

Before the end of this meeting, he suggested that I visit his factory in Hong Kong to further our business cooperation. I was pleased to hear it and promised him I would talk to Zhang Zhong about it. My one weeks' worth of time with him in Wuhan has stuck in my mind ever since. From time to time, I wonder how I ever lost contact with this Bruce Lee-like friend. Another 'what if' of my life.

A month later, I got the approval for a two-week visit to Hong Kong and then Sydney, Australia, with two of my colleagues. It was my first trip to foreign countries. Mr. Qi drove us around in Hong Kong, but the two of us had little time together, so the visit was all business.

Other than all the gleaming skyscrapers dotting both sides of the busy streets, the most distinctive difference I noticed in Hong Kong and Sydney was that most people owned cars. It was a sharp contrast to Beijing, where rivers of bicycles filled all the roads during the 1980s. And I was part of that scene, peddling through those rivers twice daily.

During the overseas trip, I witnessed the colossal gap between China and the developed world. I understood why some people in Hong Kong would instead deliberately identify themselves as not Chinese, which made Mao's ideal of socialism even more suspicious to me.

"Poverty is not socialism." Deng's words rang true. "Regardless of whether it is a white cat or a black cat, the one that catches mice is a wonderful cat." This, by far, was his most quoted catchphrase in China.

Deng's prominent apolitical stance and pragmatic approach unleashed the country's pent-up enthusiasm for wealth accumulation in the years to come. In Deng's mind, it was pointless to debate what label to give a system—whatever the "-ism," most people would try to define it. Deng's down-to-earth mien earned him genuine affection—but never idolization—from the people. One description of Deng probably caught the essence of this man: "He was an ordinary man who was dealt bad hands but turned them around amazingly." An apt analogy for Deng, who was a lifetime bridge player.

CHAPTER THIRTY-FIVE

FOR THE FIRST YEAR and a half in Beijing, I either ran around brokering business deals or idled in my bare-walled dorm room. My two large suitcases showed the wear of the New Long March that had led me all the way there. My only additional possession in Beijing was a bicycle. Every day I peddled to work and back, thirty minutes each way, rain or shine.

My ostentatious work style brought me more emptiness when I was by myself in the room filled with stillness. I knew I had been longing for something else, and I realized I could not find it where I was. It became clear that I needed to seek something outside this dorm, CEIEC, Beijing—even this country! A voice in my head nudged me to keep going.

The final reason that prompted me to act when I did was a girl, Peiyuan. We had known each other in childhood, but her family had moved to the southern city of Guangzhou. She was an outstanding student, admitted into college on the first GaoKao in 1977 with a major in biology. Even as she absorbed herself in science, she never let it get in the way of relishing life. She had a natural talent for painting and loved watching movies and getting out of the city for a day trip during the weekend. She always fit in well with friends and classmates, even as she was known to be the best student.

During our college years, we exchanged occasional letters to keep in touch. Those letters were probably dull by today's standards. It was clear to me that she and her classmates were in serious academic competition, while my classmates were more into finding suitable life partners. For her, college was a scientific undertaking, but for me, it was a process of exploration. I often shared stories with her about my extracurricular activities, like the play "Son of the Artillery Commander," in which I played the lead role. Whatever we exchanged in our letters, flirtatious expression was not part of it because it was not part of the ethos in Chinese tradition at the time.

Strange as it may seem, romance in the early 1980s in China was still unfamiliar territory for young people. Right after China's opening, the people of our generation were not really ready for imagination or romanticism. Pragmatism was a more accurate way to describe how we thought of or dealt with opposite-sex friendships or even marriage. Since Peiyuan and I both had many unknowns concerning our futures, we never even talked about what kind of future we each desired after college, let alone with whom we might like to build a life.

However, right before the last summer holiday break, she told me she and another two girls were planning to go to Shanghai for a one-week trip during the upcoming vacation. I asked if I could join them, and she said yes. During our time in Shanghai, the four of us were always together during the day, touring the city but returning to our own rooms at the end of the day. Even so, the way Peiyuan interacted with her friends had left a distinctive and profound impression on me. She did not say much, but her candor, sincerity, and sense of humor often made her friends and me laugh. Peiyuan knew that I would never be a model student like herself, but she seemed to think I was fairly good at many other things.

She and I are the same age. During the Cultural Revolution, she was sent to a Citrus Farm for three years for re-education. To me, picking oranges as a job, compared to me harvesting corn, seemed like heaven. But to her, my Daqing childhood stories and then my TianXi Production Captain experiences, including surviving the ten-day salt trip, were my highlights, which were far more intriguing to her than just going through the motions like millions of Educated Youths at the time. Our similar life experiences—overcoming adversity and catching the first wave of college entrants—played a vital role in bonding between us. She often showed off (and she still does) that she could tell which oranges were the best by simply looking at a pile of them, and I responded that I could tell time and forecast the weather by looking at the sky. Such subjects were not quite the same as a modern-day romance between girls and boys, but it was the only way for two people to be connected on a deeper level.

After graduating from university in 1982, she immediately passed the most stringent examination to become one of forty students nationwide to be accepted into the CUSBEA (China-United States Biochemistry Examination and Application) program. American professor Ray Wu had initiated the program in 1982, which lasted until 1989. Under the program, a total of 422 Ph.D. students were selected and placed in over ninety top universities in the United States. Peiyuan was admitted during its first year and eventually became one of the elite scientists in the USA.

We reconnected while I was in CEIEC. We exchanged more letters, and then phone calls. In the early 1980s, letters took about two weeks one way to arrive, and phone calls were very expensive. Her stories were totally G-rated and detailed working with other lab colleagues and her advisor during the day while relaxing with some of the two dozen Chinese scholars and students on campus. They often cooked together and went on outings like one big family during the weekend. I shared with her my entirely different, aspiring work stories in Beijing. She never suggested that I should come to the U.S. to join her because we were on such dissimilar paths—both of us full of hope but so remote in the distance. It was entirely my decision what to do next.

However, the recollection of our time together in Shanghai and from the casual letters—the feeling of being utterly free from pretension, affectation, and suspicion—made me think more about her. I began to realize that she might be the one for me. Somehow, simple biology did not play a role in choosing my life partner; if that had been the case, then I might have chosen Xiao Jun and opted for an easy and comfortable life, or ended up with HuoXing when I was lost and lonely in TianXi. Or I could have chosen someone in college like so many of my classmates who either found a dialogue partner or girls from other departments during those four years. But Peiyuan made me feel different when we were together—we never tried to impress anyone else or each other. Because we were seldom together for an extended period of time, we seemed to have a natural tacit understanding rather than explicit definitions, and that was most special to me, as no one had made me feel that way before.

Another unique part of our relationship was that Peiyuan and I were far more different than similar. Her pursuits in science were beyond my understanding, as was my passion for literature and art to her. In retrospection, we were more like two mission-driven individuals back then, designing our futures separately first and then together at last; thus, we were more a product of bizarre history and culture than of typical inner desires of youth in the Western sense. If mystery, independence, and intelligence are attractive beyond simple physical beauty, then she and I had them all! No third person became involved—not even for approval from either family. We followed our hearts, and as a result, our life together has completed us emotionally and intellectually.

I eventually told her that I had decided to apply for graduate study in the Economics Department of the University of Cincinnati, where she was now studying. We began to sketch out our future on the other side of the Pacific, where we both saw our paths would naturally cross. That was in mid-1984.

When I formally talked to my Senior VP Zhang Zhong about going to the U.S. for further study, he did not seem surprised. "Let me know if you need help getting an American visa," he said plainly, and then added, "Come back afterward because I have work for you in CEIEC."

"Yes, I will." I nodded. And I truly meant it.

Now that the official light had turned green, I had one last hurdle to overcome: passing the English test. A good score from either GRE (Graduate Record Examinations) or MET (The Michigan English Test) would suffice. I chose MET because I could schedule it anytime in Beijing (and only in Beijing).

The MET test took place in a traditional courtyard residence of a scholar from the Social Science Academy of China, Mr. Fu. He somehow administered MET from his home. With no time to waste, I scheduled my test date as soon as I could.

Mr. Fu's courtyard residence, famously known as *siheyuan*, was a four-sided composition in a historic mazelike *hutong* (a narrow alley associated with the old part of Beijing).

Siheyuan was common in old China but most famous in Beijing. The primary section always faces south, with a square courtyard in the middle that is surrounded by service rooms on both sides. The service rooms are connected to the main chamber by corridors. An ornamental double-door gate in the front leads to the main residence. The structure forms a perfect square when viewed directly from the above. The construction was fit for nobles and aristocrats in the old days.

It was almost dark when I got there. Setting my bicycle against the brick wall outside, I zipped my jacket all the way up as the evening's chill pierced through it, causing me to shiver. But I knew it was partly my nerves. Before I reached out to knock, the massive wooden gate squeaked open. In front of me stood a thin, grey-haired man wearing a pair of nearsighted glasses, which were unusually thick and heavy on his slim face.

I lowered my head and shook his hand. "Good Evening, Mr. Fu." I murmured in a voice I could hardly hear. "I'm here to take an English examination."

He led me into a service room. Through the dim light inside, I noticed a wood-burning stove in the center that radiated warmth. After I sat down on a wooden bench in front of a square table, Mr. Fu handed me a stack of papers. "This is the English test." he said. "Read it carefully before you begin, and let me know when you've completed it." I still remember the scholar's soft voice.

Burying my face deep within those pages, I felt my mind wander, picturing the American life and fantasizing about being part of it one day. When I refocused on the test, I realized that all the English I had learned was not enough to answer even half the questions. I had spent a lot of time on English in college, but mostly reading for pleasure. At this moment, when my destiny depended on it, it was too late—I couldn't figure out enough of it on the fly. Finally, I stumbled through all the questions and handed it to Mr. Fu.

He sat on the other side of the table, looking through it while I waited anxiously. He then put down the papers and talked to me as if I were his long-time student. What he said, especially the way he said it, resonates deeply within me even to this day.

He told me that when given multiple choices, some English sentences may look grammatically correct, but only one should be the right answer. Sometimes, adjectives may not be needed to describe someone or something. Most of the time, adverbs are redundant as well. With verbs, I was to choose the most potent and concise ones to get right to the point. As for prepositions, they were the most challenging part for Chinese students because they follow no obvious logic. For me, he said, the best way I could improve was to read more original English articles and pay attention to the usage conventions. "You may come and retake the test in two or three weeks." He stood up and shook my hand.

Leaving his house, I felt appreciative of his special attention. I had never learned formal English, so keeping what Mr. Fu had told me in mind, I studied almost nonstop for two weeks. I then retook the test. While he was evaluating my work, a smile appeared upon his face.

A month later, I was accepted into the Economics Department of the University of Cincinnati as a graduate student, including a scholarship to cover my full tuition, which was certainly the only way I could afford to go. One week before my flight, I received a brief letter from Mr. Fu:

Dear Cheng,

Congratulations! You will go to the U.S. to study. Could you take a moment to come to my residence before you leave?

I thought about it for a few minutes, but my mind was already far away on my upcoming journey. I tossed that letter in a drawer and never got around to it.

Decades later, after settling down in America, I often went back to China to revisit my past, looking for clues as to what has shaped my life. One time, while wandering around in Beijing, I raised my head only to find a familiar *siheyuan*. After I pushed open the squeaky wooden gate, there stood the grey-haired man wearing his thick glasses.

Sitting in that dim little room, I told Mr. Fu all about my American adventure. But when I tried to ask what he'd had on his mind to talk to me about decades ago, Mr. Fu disappeared. My eyes opened only to see the vaulted ceiling in my home in North Carolina! Mr. Fu was like a mentor I have always wished to have. Or perhaps he is the mentor who has been with me all along.

When we were young, we too often paid little attention to those who played significant roles in shaping our lives. I only realized the inattention decades later. Subsequently, I decided to use this time and place to pay tribute to the people who, by happenstance or fate, altered my life in a substantial way.

CHAPTER THIRTY-SIX

WITH EVERYTHING IN PLACE for my journey—crossing the Pacific and starting a new life—I knew I must take one last train ride back to Shenyang as a symbolic farewell to my home country. From my first train ride to TianXi, then to Dalian and, and most recently to Beijing, every time I had been on a train, I'd had the same excited feeling: I knew my physical destination, but I did not know what direction my life would take because of it. Each time I had pulled it off with luck on my side. But this time, on this train ride, my feeling of excitement came with a frisson of fear: *What would a life on the other side of the Pacific be like?*

My tangled thoughts did not last long, because a more important event was on my mind besides saying goodbye to my family: getting married to Peiyuan. She had flown to China from Cincinnati for our wedding, since having your wedding where your parents live is the custom.

We had neither time nor resources to prepare for the wedding, since I did not have much money of my own and the fall semester at U.C. had already begun. The day after we arrived, my brother and one of his friends spent an entire day preparing the wedding meal in my parents' three-room apartment. We had three tables in each room to accommodate fifteen people. A few double-happiness posters on the wall were the only sign that distinguished this occasion as a wedding.

A day later, Peiyuan and I flew to Guangzhou, where her parents were, to have a similar gathering before leaving for America.

Thinking about our wedding then, and about our daughter Cintty's wedding three decades later in America, the two weddings could not be more different. Her wedding ceremony was held in the best hotel in Raleigh, North Carolina, attended by 150 people from many parts of the U.S. and as far away as China. There was live music, an open bar, and the formal "Father of the Bride" speech—which was delivered by me. The two weddings are possibly the starkest contrast between first and second generation immigrants in our family.

It was September 1984 when my one-way flight, the ticket bought with borrowed money, deposited me on Western shores. Stepping out of the plane and setting my feet on this foreign soil, it seemed as if I had migrated to an otherworldly land. In my eagerness to embrace this new world, I now realized that I had left behind my old one. Yesterday, I'd had an envious position: I was somebody when I visited factories or received foreign visitors. Fourteen hours later, upon my arrival in the U.S, I realized that I had nothing of my own. I had to start again, from learning the language, to the systems, and even the math!

What had just happened to me? Would it all be worth it? I felt a sudden chill and shivered. My sweating hand was in my pocket, squeezing the 200 dollars in bills, which was all I had now.

Maybe Xiao Jun is right in staying where she is, I thought. My middle school and college friends had known enough to choose the life familiar to them. Yes, I wanted to know more about a new country, but I never seriously thought about what it would mean to give up the familiar one—until now! Not even the spirit of the Old Fool could pump me up this time—I had no clue where to dig. Yet, regardless of how I felt, there was no turning back now. I became a Ph.D. tracking student at the University of Cincinnati.

Thankfully, Peiyuan had arrived first. We rented a one-bedroom apartment within walking distance to U.C. We got up early in the morning and packed our lunches, often two slices of white bread ($0.50 per loaf when on sale) plus American cheese. We walked our separate ways—the medical campus for her in the Biochemistry Department and the Art and Science building for me.

While walking back and forth between my classes and my apartment, I recognized a silver Ford Granada parked along the curbside next to a familiar apartment building. A few students and I had helped a U.C. undergraduate, a girl from Taiwan, move her stuff there two weeks ago using that car. Every time I walked past it, I became more curious because the car had not moved an inch. If she does not need her car, I can definitely use one. I thought to myself, picking up the pace to my apartment.

"Hey, I see your car everyday where it is parked on the side of the street. If you do not need it anymore, then how about selling it to me?" I said to her over the phone.

"Okay, you can have it for 300 dollars." She said it straight-forwardly.

"It's a deal! I'm coming over right now."

Three hundred dollars for a car! I hit my forehead with the phone before hanging up, wondering if it might be a dream. For someone who had been born, raised, and lived in the bicycle world, I thought I had struck gold! This 1975 Ford Granada, with its shining red leather interior, was exceptionally smooth on the road. Two months after I had landed in this part of the world, I suddenly felt like I had stumbled one step closer to the famed American way of life, now on four wheels.

I asked an older graduate student to help me get the car and show me how to drive. He let me take the wheel and pointed to the expressway after ten minutes on a local road. Cruising at seventy miles per hour, I was on a flying carpet! From my life in Beijing with no air conditioning, no kitchen, no bathroom—not even tap water—inside my dorm room, this transition was no less dramatic than taking a time machine to a futuristic world.

It didn't last for long, though. I was back to my desk, facing a stack of textbooks, when reality set in again. I had arrived late for the first semester. That, plus my lack of basic math and no history of academic training, were like several mountains placed in front of me. But I had to move them, because there was no other way.

To my astonishment, I scored two As, and the rest Bs, at the end of my first semester! Once again, I thought: maybe this pig can fly.

Chapter Thirty-seven

Two weeks after I received my driver's license, one of my U.C. friends arranged an interview for me with a Chinese restaurant to deliver food—a perfect opportunity to put my newly acquired skill to lucrative use.

I immediately said yes and drove to the restaurant, Oriental Kitchen, to meet the owner. He was a fit-looking, middle-aged man, who had immigrated from Taiwan. His family name was Li, so I called him Li Laoban (boss). His wife wore full makeup and flashy dresses, as if she were about to go onstage for a show. She sat on a coach seat, sipping tea, never taking a moment to glance at the people passing through their door.

Scanning me up and down, Li Laoban's practiced eyes could tell that I was a young man fresh off the boat from the Mainland, in his view a backward and oppressive part of China. Thus, a life lesson would be imperative before putting me to work. As I recall, Li Laoban did not ask me any questions—it was as if he already knew me. Instead, he began by telling his personal story, with a genial intent to convert this young Maoist into a libertarian, I imagined.

"When I was fifteen years old," he opened, "I came to this country and worked as a busboy in the evenings while going to school during the day. Later, I became a waiter and finally, a chef. After college, I continued to labor ten hours a day, six days a week. It was fifteen years before I could open this restaurant." He said it all while looking quite serious. "If you are willing to put in hard work, this country will provide you a comfortable life," he concluded. I nodded in admiration. This was my first job interview ever, which turned out to include my first true immigrant story in America.

A notable wave of immigrants from Taiwan to the U.S. occurred in the 1970s, more than a decade earlier than when the people from Mainland China started to arrive. In our eyes, the Taiwanese who emigrated to America were all well off (like the Taiwanese girl who sold me her car). But not all of them were, apparently, like Li Laoban. Many had had to start from the very bottom to earn a basic living, working their way up to enjoy a better life.

"Can you drive a car with a manual transmission?" Li Laoban asked me, pointing his chin toward an old Subaru hatchback parked outside the restaurant.

"Sure," I replied. But really I had no idea. I figured a car was a car, as implied by my driver's license—manual or otherwise. Mostly, I just wanted the job.

Apparently, he did not sense my lack of confidence (I had never even touched a car with a manual transmission). "You can come back in two hours, when mealtime starts." Before finishing his last word, Li Laoban had already turned his back to return to the kitchen.

I was thrilled, and dashed home to change into more comfortable clothes for my first paying job in America.

When I showed up to start work, Li Laoban handed me a car key, a brown bag with a receipt stapled to its top, and a piece of paper with a hand-written address on it. "Here you go. It's four blocks from here." Getting into the car, I remembered seeing Master Li back in TianXi driving the Grand Liberation. I had always been curious about the manual truck, and was even tempted to try it. Now it was my turn.

I drove the car out of the parking lot easily enough, since it was slightly downhill. After making my first turn, I stopped at the red light. But when I wanted to go at the green light, the clutch and gas pedals refused to work together. The car, under my clumsy feet, was unwilling to move forward. Seeing the cars lined up behind me only made matters worse. Had I been too careless in taking this job? Just as I reached the peak of my frustration, a young American stopped his car and walked over to me. "Do you need help?" he asked.

I rolled down the window. "I can't get this car moving because it has a manual transmission, and I don't know how..."

"It happens to everyone on their first time." He smiled, which made me feel immensely relieved. He told me to press the clutch down so he could push the car to the side of the road. He then sat in the passenger seat for about twenty minutes, explaining to me how to use a manual transmission. He suggested that I practice a while on the road until I could manage it. "Just take it easy. You will get better at it soon." He smiled and stepped out.

"Thank you so much," I said.

After years of living in America, I learned from my own experiences and from others, that it was common for strangers to stop and offer help, such as when someone was having car trouble on the road. Such a simple courtesy, however, was—and still is—uncommon in China.

Needless to say, my first delivery on my first day at my first American job did not go well. It took me a full hour to return to the restaurant.

"Why have you been out for so long?" Li Laoban was clearly in a grumpy mood.

"I got a little lost in that neighborhood. And the car..."

I stopped short of telling him what had happened. Li Laoban seemed to have another lecture for me, but as it reached his lips, he let it slide, realizing that I was just starting a new life in a new country. However, when I came back to work the following day, I noticed the same Subaru was no longer in its parking spot. Instead, Li Laoban's family van was parked there. I asked the waitress about the hatchback. "That car was having trouble with its transmission and was towed away to a repair shop this morning," she told me.

I immediately surmised that the "trouble" must have been the result of what I had done to the car the previous day. I felt immensely guilty, mostly because I had kept quiet about what had actually happened. However, for the next few years in Cincinnati, while I no longer needed to work part-time, I always came to cover a shift for Li Laoban each time he called. He opened two more restaurants during the time I was in Cincinnati. He told me more about his life in America and his restaurant stories. And he always told me to take home whatever food I liked for my wife each time I left his restaurant.

I had heard about successful immigrants in America. But now I had one as my friend, a self-made capitalist. I saw no sign of a dark soul, but rather a hard-working human being who came in at 9:00 am and left at 10:00 pm, six days a week, year-round. People like him are not parasites, but the pillars of the economy.

"Among every three people, there must be a teacher," Confucius said in Analytics. Li Laoban was one for me.

CHAPTER THIRTY-EIGHT

A week before my second semester started, a letter from my Department arrived:

We have selected you to be a T.A. (Teaching Assistant). You will receive a living stipend of $550.00 a month starting in the spring semester.

Reading this letter, I could not believe my eyes, especially the number. Only a few months earlier in Beijing, my monthly salary was equivalent to only twenty dollars, even with a privileged job. I would have had to work for two and a half years to have that much money in my pocket. And now, I was being paid that much to carry a few books while classroom hopping.

I was now an official T.A. in the Economics Department, assisting a professor with his undergraduate teachings; an enormous honor for someone with one semester of economics education. It was a distant dream that had come true much sooner than I had expected. Maybe I know more than I think I know, I speculated.

Acquiring such financial assistance was a significant load off my mind. From that moment on, my journey in this magical land became less treacherous. I immediately quit delivering food, except as an occasional favor for Li Laoban, and became entirely focused on Western economics—the very reason I'd come here in the first place. I wanted to learn about this economic theory, one which definitely conflicted with my indoctrination during my years in China.

"Learning something new is hard, but unlearning is actually much harder," I thought to myself each time I wrestled with both sides of the argument that seemed to oppose each other. Here before me was Western economics, a theory based on the assumption that greed is an inherent human trait; that an 'economic person' must act rationally in his own self-interest, seeking to maximize his own utility (or profit). Because of this universal trait, competition was forged, productivity was heightened, human satisfaction could be boosted, and society would thrive.

Western economic theory totally contradicted Marxist theory, which stated that the same essential trait in all of us would lead to class-warfare: an unavoidable consequence of greed in a capitalist society.

There's no denying that the Western economics proved to be correct. America was definitely more advanced and prosperous than China. That I already owned an automobile and lived in a climate-controlled apartment with wall-to-wall carpets said it all.

Was Marx wrong about his profit theory? Or how to resolve the frictions between those that have and those that do not? I sought answers.

Then, my first experience of real "culture shock" allowed me to take in another version of human nature.

"What movies do you like?" our American landlord asked me one day.

"War and action," I told him.

He recommended *First Blood*. Growing up in a conformist culture, following the group and trying to fit in was the only norm I had known. Rambo left me with eyes wide open the entire time. This movie, which had the best action and war scenes I had ever seen, blurred the line between virtue and evil. Even the villains, like the Sheriff and his Deputy, saw themselves as justified, which contrasted markedly with traditional Chinese literature and it depicted a culture of uncompromised individualism. One man fought for what was right for himself, even against an entire army!

Rambo, among many iconic Hollywood figures, became my American idol. I followed him—on and off the screen—till his *Last Blood*. Other than the entertaining aspects of the movies, Rambo's survival escapades provided me with a new perception of a universal man: full of flesh and blood and emotion, instead of the cold 'economic man' who acted only rationally and uniformly, driven solely by edict.

Money or profit as a motivator does play a critical role in civilization. But to what extent does it do so for an individual (especially a well-balanced one) in modern society? Should the multifaceted nature in all of us, particularly our emotions—valuing what is right and defending it at any cost—be a closer representation of true human beings than a highly-simplified one? In a long quest to answer my questions and satisfy my debate over Marx's profit theory versus Western economics, I came to realize that we human beings were—and still are—part of a mystery that modern economists have yet to solve. And perhaps they never will! Or is there some science that will someday provide a generalized answer? This realization put an end to my personal quandary, if not to the essential puzzle, by leaving it unsolved.

CHAPTER THIRTY-NINE

WHILE MY INTELLECTUAL EXPERIENCE in America was stimulating and rewarding, our student life (Peiyuan's and mine) in Cincinnati could not have been any more idyllic, which we have often reminisced about in later years. During my five-plus years as a graduate student in Cincinnati (Peiyuan stayed two years longer in her post-doctorate position), we together received $1,300 monthly assistance, more than enough to cover anything we needed in those days. Weekdays, she went to her lab, and I hung out in the library, scanning newspapers and magazines or immersing myself for hours in the study of modern economics. We often made a deliberate effort in planning our weekends: we would start by looking at a map to discover a large green area, preferably one with a lake in the middle or a river running through it. We would load our car with a big cooler full of drinks, fruits, cooked meats, and cold beers, and then commune with nature for a restful day.

During school breaks—spring, summer, and winter—we tried to see part of the country; we even ventured into Canada occasionally. We often went with other family friends for those longer trips, bringing tents to camp along the way, even a rice cooker to accommodate our Chinese diet.

I soon realized that the degree of happiness was relative, and the law of diminishing marginal rate of return, as I'd learned in my economics classes, made the most sense in theory as well as in life. Which means only that the additional, or "marginal," return or satisfaction (rather than the total return or satisfaction) truly matters, and it will diminish as you have more of it.

For example, after a sweaty workout under the blistering sun, one's first sip of cold beer feels most gratifying, while the last sip of the third bottle could taste drab by comparison. Similarly, I have changed cars more often than I can count over the decades, and each time the new car is better than the previous one. Still, I cherish the memory of my first $300 car the most, as if it were a first love—admittedly imperfect, but still unforgettable.

In the meantime, my academic life became equally invigorating. My adviser, Dr. Wolfgang, was in his early fifties. He was already bald, and his piercing blue eyes behind a pair of black-framed glasses made him a perfect cartoonist's caricature of a genuine scholar. He was the most respected economist in our Department and well-known in his field, but exceptionally easy-going and compassionate. To me, he was as much an academic adviser as a life mentor. As an immigrant from Austria, he had never applied for U.S. citizenship (I now wish I had asked him the reason for that). More than all our other professors, he took particular care of the foreign students (there were quite a few in our Department). He understood better than most what these students went through by coming to America: dramatic changes academically, yes, but even more so culturally.

The way he taught in our graduate classes was amazing. He would write out everything he lectured about on the blackboard. He talked slowly and distinctively, but wrote fast and lucidly. My eyes, ears, and hand on the writing pad worked correspondingly without pause, except during the discussion sessions. And I always felt that I had thoroughly captured what he had taught us on my writing pad.

Conversing with Dr. Wolfgang was always enlightening and fun. Every two weeks, I would think of a reasonable excuse to see him. For my degree, I had chosen to develop a mathematical model to further growth theory analysis, but it was outside his experience on international economics. Despite that, he encouraged me fully and even referred me to a mathematics professor in the Aerospace Engineering Department.

As a result of my graduate studies, I had gained a different and more in-depth understanding of economic analysis and the similarities between social sciences and natural science. More particularly, I had learned how one field could borrow techniques from another to illustrate its own theory better. Somehow, I now found that math was not quite so tedious and dull as I'd once thought it to be.

After completing the required classes and passing the Ph.D. qualifications at the end of my second year, I had a shared office with two other graduate students. All I needed to do was read papers for my dissertation and get an assistantship for it. The first part of my motto, striving for an 'intellectual mind,' seemed to take shape now, by my own standard, at least.

Although I never conceived of economics as a profession, its impact on me—on my examination of perspectives across cultures—has proved to be more than words can describe. I cherished my time in Cincinnati for being the only genuine schooling I ever received.

And I now started my days with a freshly-brewed cup of coffee—instead of tea—because all the professors would have a cup of java in their hands anywhere, anytime I met them. I believe the axiom "when in Rome, do as the Romans do" because it was really the only way to achieve a true sense of belonging. My cup of joe first thing in the morning became a daily rite; and I later understood that this simple shift from tea to coffee symbolically underscored a culture-crossing expedition.

CHAPTER FORTY

OUR BLISSFUL YEARS IN Cincinnati, embellished by our new life on four wheels, whizzed by like the scenery outside my car window while driving down the freeway. Fast-forwarding to 1988, I found myself once again standing at a crossroads.

One day, a letter appeared in my mailbox from Zhang Zhong, my Senior V.P. at CEIEC. He had been in New York for two years in charge of all the CEIEC business and foreign affairs of North America. He invited me to visit him in New Haven, Connecticut, during my upcoming spring break.

My two years working at CEIEC had been transitory but eventful, leaving me fond memories of both the places and the people with whom I had worked. Zhang Zhong, more than any other, had had the most positive influence on me, as he had helped me to get my U.S. visa.

Peiyuan and I would never pass up a chance to get away for a few days, so I gladly accepted his invitation.

By that time, we had upgraded to a 1980 Mazda 323 hatchback, which cost us $1,000—a sleek-looking and fuel-efficient car. Only a few months ago, my 1975 Granada had been taken over by a new Chinese student coming to The Conservatory of Music of U.C., a young violinist. I helped him to settle into his dorm. He then mentioned he needed a car to work part-time. He was very envious of my $300 car.

In his eyes, our financial situation was better than most Chinese students at U.C. Acting like a little brother, he nudged me to get a newer and better car so he could have the Granada. I can't deny that the Granada was special to me, but I gave in, telling him to take good care of it. Like a jackpot winner, he dashed into a nearby

McDonald's and returned with Quarter Pounders, plus super-sized everything, for the two of us to celebrate the purchase of his first car.

I could hardly wait to take this newly-acquired Mazda for a long, leisurely ride. Throwing everything we could think of into the back of the car, we steered onto the American superhighway.

———

Zhang Zhong and his wife resided in a quaint, English Tudor nestled in tranquil surroundings in New Haven. Its characteristic stucco exterior, exposed timbers, and pitched gable roof made it seem as if we had stepped into a European vista. While I was admiring the house's design, the front door opened.

"Hey, Xiao Wang!" Zhang Zhong greeted me in a familiar voice.

"Hello, Zhang Zhong. How are you? This is my wife, Peiyuan."

We followed him into the house. Zhang Zhong's wife was in the kitchen. She was in her mid-forties, ten years younger than Zhang Zhong. She had a way of conveying genial hospitality—not in words, but through her warm eyes and affable smile, making us feel right at home. We called her Zhang TaiTai (Mrs. Zhang).

"You both must be thirsty, so have some fruit before dinner," she said, presenting a big plate piled high with oranges, pears, and apples. Two glasses of hot tea appeared in front of us.

We thanked her, and Zhang Zhong then led us to our own bedroom, a cozy, inviting, and perfect place to rest up after our ten-hour drive. Sensing my curiosity, Zhang Zhong said, "CEIEC leased the house for us." In my head, I was already sketching out our future American life, and this place could easily have fit in as a part of that picture.

Our dinner was informal, yet delightful, all at the hands of Zhang TaiTai. In Chinese tradition, only the closest friends or relatives would be treated with home-made meals in one's private residence. I felt privileged that Zhang Zhong thought of me as someone beyond the superior-subordinate relationship. Instead, ours was more like a special bond between an elder and a junior.

After two rounds of Moutai, a brand of baijiu usually reserved for special occasions, Zhang Zhong's voice became serious. "After one more year in New York, I will go back to CEIEC in Beijing, to become the president of the newly-reformed and a much larger multinational conglomerate," he said in his usual slow and distinctive fashion. After a pause, he continued, "CEIEC differs completely from the time when you were in Beijing—because China is vastly different now. It is like a jumbo jet: fueled and ready to take off. All the policies are in place, and they are aimed at one thing only—to grow as fast as possible."

"Congratulations, Zhang Zhong!" I raised my cup of Moutai. The two cups clinked together.

I had not been following what was happening in China during my four years in Cincinnati, and now Zhang Zhong filled that enormous gap in for me. I remained pensive as I contemplated the meaning of the exciting developments taking place in China.

"We are in our best time ever," Zhang Zhong added, "but we are badly in need of the right people to take the lead in the major areas. I'm looking for people who have the proper training and seek progressively higher goals, rather than those who are simply content with a comfortable life: people who can take CEIEC into the modern era." His face lit up, and I was certain I looked the same way, inspired by his vision. "I will work at least another five years in Beijing: five golden years to put my ideas into practice before passing the helm to someone else."

I was admittedly so out of touch with the advancements taking place in China that I was just trying to visualize the massive picture he was drawing before me.

"What is your current plan, Xiao Wang?" He then raised his eyes to mine. "Have you ever thought about going back to Beijing... to work with me?" He pressed onward before I even had the time to consider the idea. "If you can assist me, we will leave a mark on CEIEC, on China's entire electronics industry, by promoting it to the world." His message could not have been more candid.

His proposition was a shock to me, because I had never given serious thought to what I would do after leaving U.C. Then again, it was not too big a surprise, because CEIEC was the only place I had ever worked, and it was a career I prized, and Zhang Zhong had always held a special place in my memory. I lowered my head to chew on the idea of going back to China in such a historical time, along with Zhang Zhong's trust in me to take on this significant responsibility.

"Peiyuan will soon complete her Ph.D., but I am still working on my dissertation, which will take two to three years to complete." I was truthfully chronicling my progress. "I can get a master's degree anytime, though, and continue working on my dissertation anywhere." As I defined my situation, I felt my enthusiasm, which had lain dormant for years, reawaken. My heart was racing now. "I will go back to Beijing with you, Zhang Zhong." I ended it firmly, raising my cup, and we clinked again.

Could my unequivocal decision have been partly of the effect of a little too much baijiu? I reflected on it later, thinking about the commitment that could alter our future—both mine and Peiyuan's—forever. And, at that point in time, Peiyuan and I had not even talked about it.

Deep down, getting a Ph.D. in economics did not actually pique my interest. I had always enjoyed being active, and could not imagine focusing on a theoretical field for my entire life. Economic theory was too hypothetical, in my opinion, to be practically useful. As for our family, Peiyuan and I had an entire year to figure it out, and we'd always shared a common understanding in making vital decisions.

The next day, Zhang Zhong took us to his office in New York, high in one of the World Trade Center towers. There were six people sent here from CEIEC to work, and I knew them all from the old days. We had a good time chatting. Mostly, though, I felt like they were all nearly the same as they had been in Beijing, although they were now in New York.

They spent most of their time either at the office or in their apartments in New Haven. I heard more than a couple of times how lucky I was, having the freedom to go anywhere I desired. I did not know if they had specific orders not to do anything else or lacked the means and interest to venture outside of their workplaces. Possibly both, I supposed.

After a two-night stay in Connecticut, Peiyuan and I drove back to Cincinnati mostly in silence. Standing at a crossroads, I now felt a deep sense of purpose and was eager to dive back into the affairs of my home country now that it had come calling. And the timing could not have been better: like getting on the initial flight of a jumbo jet right before take-off, as Zhang Zhong had put it. Undoubtedly, Western economics was what China needed most to further its reform, and I could be the one to introduce them to its possibilities.

Coming back to U.C., I spent most of my time catching up on the political and economic developments in China—instead of cultivating hypothetical economic models for my dissertation. What could be more meaningful, I asked, than putting the Western theories and principles I had assimilated into practice in China in order to modernize a still backward country, and to make an impact on my native land? I felt more alive than I had at any time in the past.

CHAPTER FORTY-ONE

NINETEEN EIGHTY-NINE WAS the year that reshuffled the cards of the world order. It presented the first significant challenge to the reformation policies and opening of China, and completely redrew my roadmap once more.

An anti-socialism revolutionary wave crashed through Eastern and Central Europe, projecting an obvious influence upon this Eastern Middle Kingdom.

On January 20, 1989, George H. W. Bush was sworn in as the 41st President of the United States. Following Ronald Reagan's famous "Tear down this wall" speech that challenged Soviet leader Gorbachev to open Eastern Europe, George H. W. Bush ensured the final break-up of the Soviet bloc, ending the Cold War on November 9, 1989.

On February 6, the Solidarity Union in Poland became a significant movement. It forced the Polish government to hold formal talks with its representatives for the first time since 1981. On June 4 of the same year, Solidarity was legalized and allowed to participate in semi-free elections. Tadeusz Mazowiecki of Solidarity, the first non-Communist in forty-two years, was elected as Prime Minister of Poland, marking the end of communist control of the country.

On March 15, mass demonstrations in Hungary demanded democracy. It was the first crack to appear in the Iron Curtain. In late October, Hungary's parliament adopted legislation that provided direct presidential elections and multi-party parliamentary elections.

March 26 marked the first contested elections that the Soviet Union had held for its parliament. The Congress of People's Deputies of the Soviet Union, which marked the beginning of the end of socialism in Eastern and Central Europe, led to the Fall of the Berlin Wall on November 9, 1989. The notorious Cold War was at an end.

This same anti-socialism tidal wave from Central and Eastern Europe reached Asia and rippled throughout China.

Deng had sounded the horn of economic reform in the early 1980s, which shook every corner of the country, both politically and economically. But no one knew how to draw up clear policies to smoothly move this idea forward, not even Deng himself (as he openly admitted). Lack of theoretical guidance meant a lack of practical policies for dealing with the relationship between public and private ownership, as well as the relationship between the central and local governments. These two issues together—exacerbated by a lack of moral construct—blurred the lines between the legal and illegal, providing hotbeds for corruption to spread.

"We could expand our business in almost any way we want in China," Zhang Zhong had said to me, which I did not quite understand until one year later, in 1989. By that time, one major obstacle had emerged to slow down—if not derail—the reform: the two-track pricing system. It aimed to control the most important industrial and agricultural products at the government's fixed prices, but to leave everyday necessities to be determined by the market.

This two-track pricing system provided a breeding ground for corruption, and undermined the incentives to produce government-controlled products. Therefore, it caused hyperinflation in the marketplace. To solve the problem, the government adopted a policy to increase the money supply, but that only further exacerbated inflation and corruption.

Facing growing chaos and lax regulations, all attempts to boost the economy failed. Unemployment skyrocketed, while inflation, which had reached eighteen percent in 1987, climbed to twenty-seven percent in the following year. Dissatisfaction with the status quo steadily grew, brewing the desire for social justice. Influenced by similar movements in Central and Eastern Europe, Chinese intellectuals began to openly criticize the corrupt political and economic structures and demand further political reforms. Timing is everything, but only if something is meant to happen. This time, a series of successful revolutionary movements in Eastern and Central Europe had been a godsend, deepening fundamental reforms in China—at least, that was how it appeared at first.

If China was ripe for change...

CHAPTER FORTY-TWO

ON APRIL 15, 1989, Hu Yaobang (former General Secretary of the CCP from 1981 to 1987) died in China. Following his death, residents and students amassed to hold various memorial services. This later sparked the protests that began in Tiananmen Square, mostly by university students in Beijing, which spread to other major cities in China. According to reports, one million people had assembled in Tiananmen Square at the height of the protests. This movement set in motion the political turmoil that would later become known as the June 4 Tiananmen Square Incident. As we know, the protests were subdued by troops advancing into central parts of Beijing in the early morning of June 4, causing the deaths of both demonstrators and bystanders in the process.

That afternoon, on June 4, Peiyuan and I watched CNN with three U.C. Chinese friends. We were stunned by the images of the burnings, gunshots, and tanks roaring into Tiananmen Square. And then, the iconic voice from former President Ronald Reagan: "You cannot massacre an idea," the former president said in a speech during a private visit to Britain. "You cannot run tanks over hope. You cannot riddle a people's yearning with bullets. Those heroic Chinese students who gave their lives have released the spirit of democracy and it cannot be called back. That spirit is loose upon the world this spring."

I stood up and suggested that we each pack a small bag right away and drive to the Chinese Embassy in Washington D.C. to let our voices be heard.

Thirty minutes later, five of us crammed into my little car, and we were on our way to D.C. Well past midnight, we arrived in the capital city. Five weary travelers crashed at a friend's apartment on the living room floor and awaited the dawn to hit Pennsylvania Avenue.

When we reached the central district the next morning, a river of people already lined the famous avenue. All had arrived spontaneously, just like us. There were no organizers, no social media, and no one to tell the crowd what to do or how we should do it.

The crowd gathered in front of Capitol Hill. We marched and shouted with arms waving all the way to the front plaza of the Chinese Embassy. The Embassy's gate remained locked, as if a deluge of demonstrators was expected and was about to gush into the building.

In the crowd, we ran into a few of our college friends who had come from other cities. We then went to the nearby China Town to have Peking duck for lunch together. The atmosphere became subdued, but clear: we were not against the culture in which we grew up—that was who we were—but we despised the brutal measures that had been taken. We knew we were lucky to be on this side of the Pacific: we could "watch the fire across the river" and freely convey our genuine emotions.

The Chinese official newspaper, *People's Daily*, stated that the decision to give the order to march troops into Tiananmen Square to quell the riots was made by the CCP Central Committee, the State Council, and the Central Military Commission. Deng Xiaoping was the Chairman of the Central Military Commission.

Following that event, Feng Qi turned dramatically. In an overwhelming bit of symmetry, it had shattered my desire to go back to serve the country, almost as if a light had switched off in my head. Once again, Deng's ruling had abruptly altered my future.

Zhang Zhong was called back to Beijing shortly afterward in accordance with the CCP, and we lost contact. For me, going back to CEIEC or China was now entirely out of the question. Deep down, I felt like a boy who had run away from home, and I didn't want, or dare, to look back.

And yes, China had been like a one-billion-person household, all relying on the wise elders to make significant decisions. That was deeply rooted in the culture all along. From time to time, in that expansive household, there were a few runaways like me, but the majority of those who have remained in their chosen land and have lived their lives peacefully and mostly content.

Obviously, China did not follow in the footsteps of Central and

Eastern Europe. And certainly it did not adopt most Western values—those widely considered to be science-based, as opposed to the tradition-driven values often seen in Asia.

Was it China's approach to represent Eastern values by another name? Were Eastern traditions by any definition backward, submissive, or inferior? Would defending the status quo largely represent the idea of a "socialist market economy with Chinese characteristics" that Deng had pictured in his mind? Was Deng's vision of a hybrid economic system, in which a state-owned enterprise sector (market socialism) existed alongside a private ownership sector (market capitalism), the right approach for China?

Only time would tell...

CHAPTER FORTY-THREE

MY NOW COMPROMISED ASPIRATIONS to return to China and work in the service of my native country left me at a loss for direction. Anything related to my home country now felt like rubbing salt into an open wound. I purposely tried to avoid subjects related to it, such as its people, current events, movies, and Spring Festivals. For a few months, I couldn't find my compass or get my mind to focus on my academic work.

Overwhelmed by my doubt and angst, I questioned, "Where can I call home?"

Burying my head in the sand did not help, because I could not escape from my frequent moments of introspection and self-consciousness. These moments, somehow, often led me to think of Deng Xiaoping again. Thanks to him, my homeland had become hopeful for the first time in my life, and I was now on a course once beyond imagination. Furthermore, Deng's determination toward carrying out economic reform was still unwavering, if not more resolute.

In November of 1989, Deng resigned from his position as the Chairman of the Central Military Commission. But that did not slow him down in pushing forward his economic policies. Shortly thereafter, Deng visited Shanghai. "Speed up constructing Pudong, and do not waver until completion," he urged Shanghai officials. "The people of Shanghai should be more open and liberated, acting bolder and pushing forward harder."

Pudong has since expanded the size of the original Shanghai by a quarter in only twenty years (amassing another six million in population). It is a miraculous metropolis rising from paddy fields, otherwise known as the Pearl of the Orient.

Subconsciously, my decision not to return never stopped my

heart from returning from time to time. Years later, our family has acquired a lovely second home in Pudong (did this decision have anything to do with Deng again? I sometimes muse on this milestone in our family life). Shanghai is no longer a mere stopover in China, but rather a solid foothold—another home for our family. With two windows to peek at both sides of the Pacific, I feel the shifts of Feng Qi in real-time.

Deng Xiaoping left his successors a famous "28-Character Strategy" (28 Chinese words or characters) in the early 1990s:

"Observe calmly; secure our position; cope with affairs calmly; hide our capabilities and bide our time; maintain a low profile; never take the lead; and make some contribution."

These words have guided Chinese foreign policy for years. More importantly, they summed up Deng's own life. Among those words, 'never take the lead' was the most profound, and the most difficult to abide for any powerful man or country. But Deng himself had done it, as he never desired to be the country's top leader, much less be idolized, like Mao had in his era.

When people openly referred to Deng as "Comrade Xiaoping," leaving off his last name and official titles, it illustrated the sense of intimacy that the public felt for him. No other top Chinese leader has ever come close. Nevertheless, his decisive measure to end the June 4 incident at Tiananmen Square had displayed another side of him. He was who he was, and like any iron-willed leader, Deng knew exactly where he drew his line in the sand. Whatever the world would think of Deng: as a prominent communist leader, Maoism defender, fearless reformer, architect of modern China, or a combination of all these elements, they may have missed the central point of his life. Deng was, above all, a man with a big heart. He did something for the country and followed it all the way through in a way no one could have imagined.

The life of this Educated Youth (like millions of others) was shaped and re-shaped by Deng's decisions each time I found myself at a crossroad. I never believed in supernatural powers, but what other way was there to explain the propitious pattern of occurrences? A mere consequence of coincidences or dumb luck did not seem to cut it. It felt as if someone must have conspired to play me like a marionette, making me perform in a way I never knew I could. But every step seemed to be inevitable.

Regardless of what I would call the ostensibly disconnected pieces that have paved the way for me, I slowly and finally realized: I could settle in this faraway land and call it my home—my adopted home.

Decades later, when China was far more developed, people who knew of my past often wondered: "What if you had returned to China to work with Zhang Zhong in 1989?" making it sound like I had missed a once-in-a-lifetime opportunity to partake in China's wealth-building craze. With Deng's directive in my mind—"observe calmly; secure our position; cope with affairs calmly; hide our capabilities and bide our time; maintain a low profile; never take the lead; and make some contribution"—I simply softly chuckled and offered no comment.

Mere wealth was never a driver for me. I knew that was never enough. Besides, I now had more than I'd ever thought I needed. Plus, living in America granted me the freedom to explore, and even to fail, which was not only liberating, but something that no amount of wealth could replace.

In February 1997, Deng Xiaoping died at the age of ninety-three. He will forever be remembered as a person short in stature (height: five feet, two inches) but as a towering figure in history.

Chapter Forty-four

Once the ache for returning home had diminished, my mind was freed and a new life emerged. My destiny is finally in my own hands, I thought to myself, recognizing that I was already where I had always wanted to be. Therefore, nothing seemed as appealing as turning this adopted country into my primary home.

And I soon discovered unlimited options to explore in this diverse melting pot. But simply being in the pot guaranteed nothing, unless one was willing to be 'melted' first. And all that took was for me to be open and ready to embrace this novel way of life: a culture like no other on earth.

It was, in fact, easy to fall in love with my new home—a place free of community nagging, cultural concerns, and even traditional obligations because of the twelve-hour time difference between my parents and siblings, and myself. A place where I could finally become who I wanted to be…

On paper, I was now an American citizen. Just as I had dreamed when I prepared for GaoKao decades ago. I finally broke away from a rigid structure and embraced an open and boundless world. I now had a blank page upon which to draw.

In 1988 in Cincinnati, Peiyuan and I welcomed a lovely daughter. We named her Cintty to commemorate the university and our foster city, which had unconditionally accepted us. We then moved to New Jersey in late 1989, where Peiyuan was offered a post-doctorate position. I worked in an international trading firm for three years before Peiyuan received an offer from a major pharmaceutical company in Research Triangle Park, North Carolina.

Peiyuan and I were enamored with the ambiance of the area during our first visit to North Carolina. The whole of Research Triangle Park was nestled deep in the woods, soothing and serene compared to the never-ending noise in northern New Jersey. Most of the single-family houses were tucked away within the planned subdivisions. They were spacious, safe, and most of all, quiet. The desire to live in one place—rather than uprooting our life once every few years—settled within me for the first time. We decided to plant our roots there, and in 1992, we started to look for our first house in Cary, North Carolina.

Having only been in Cary a few months, Peiyuan and I did not know anyone. We found a construction site with a dozen homesites plotted out. We went into the modular shelter that served as the sales office where we met Chris, the site agent. He was six feet, four inches tall with a slim body and a shy smile. Knowing that we were looking for our first home, he unfolded all the papers on the table to show us everything he had.

"Do you have an agent working for you?" Chris asked.

"No, we did not know anyone," I said. Suddenly, I realized this would be a considerable gain for the builder. "But I expect you to make it up to us, since you don't have to worry about an agent commission," I added.

"No problem." Chris agreed happily.

We then picked one of the floor plans and a home site. We signed the contract right there: the first place we ever visited on our first day of searching. Over the seven months of building that house, Peiyuan and I went to see Chris every other week to pick over the options, while Chris added plenty of upgrades to the house for free. I brought him some exotic Chinese snacks every time we visited (all agents liked to snack, I noticed, since they seem to have too much time to themselves), and he took me on duck hunting trips with his friends.

That house cost us $155,000 for its 2,600 square feet: roomy and comfortable. After I got to know several neighbors and friends living nearby, I learned that our first house had ended up as the best deal in the neighborhood. Purchasing this first house felt similar to my first ($300!) car. Was I just lucky or what?

Unfortunately, that year coincided with the ongoing economic recession; therefore, not everything was smooth sailing. While Peiyuan worked in the pharmaceutical industry, I started a company of my own, but it did not pan out as I had expected. As it turned out, this excellent place for family life was not necessarily a great place to start a business. And the downturn of the economy only made it worse. But slow business for me meant more time to pay attention to the things that piqued my curiosity.

Theoretically, an economic downturn was nothing new to me. But it was my first taste of what a Western economic recession was like; most of all, how people from various social and cultural backgrounds reacted to it.

The 1992 economic recession was triggered by a tightening policy to fight inflation, coupled with an oil price shock. Even after the GDP had turned the corner, consequences such as sinking property values and lackluster investment incentives lingered for a few years. According to one report, the average American family consequentially experienced a fifty-three percent increase in credit card debt.

Yet, when I looked around at the Chinese community, I saw people acting like nothing had happened, even for those who had lost jobs. On a typical day, they would send their children to school in the morning, then to Chinese school or ballet, piano, tennis, or swimming lessons in the afternoon. They would then come home to prepare the family meal in the early evening, and play card or ball games with their Chinese friends before going to bed.

Weekends were often a rotation of potluck parties, which could easily exceed ten families each time. Socializing was mostly confined within the community. That summed up a simplistic, but mostly unruffled way of life in America. It was a painless way to get through the economic hills and valleys.

Delving into the melting pot, I have noticed two different ways of treating money. For some, all money—whether it is hard-earned, a one-time bonus, a gift, or a credit card—is regarded as fungible. Which means money is money: worthy of the same, and thus deserving the same care; therefore, all money should be spent with equal rationality.

Another way is to splurge a one-time bonus on a big family vacation or a major appliance, even a new car, treating it as easy money. Credit cards, especially, are used far more freely than cash, as though it were other people's money. And we all know what happens after credit card debt piles up.

With different mindsets toward money comes different ways to manage family debts. Chinese people I knew used credit cards whenever they could, but made full payments at the end of the month. This one habit usually led to better credit scores, and thus lower mortgage rates. These debts were more manageable, even in bad economic times.

Foreclosures are the daily headlines in the aftermath of every financial crisis, the worst of them being the housing market crash in 2008. Chinese families mostly managed to avoid it.

Somehow, this seemingly simple idea is not an easy one to pass along. Credit cards did not even exist in China before the year 2000, and I got my first credit card after "melting" into the American way of life in Cincinnati. Long before that, the Confucian "Doctrine of the Mean" had sowed its seeds in the 'collective' psyche.

Confucius conveyed the following truth in *Analects*: "The virtue embodied in the Doctrine of the Mean is of the highest order. But it has long been rare among people. One should do everything in moderation or within the means. 'Overdoing' is as bad as 'under-doing.'" Thus, it is all about "mastering the inches," as the old Chinese saying goes.

No one ever gives Confucius credit for keeping people out of financial troubles in today's live now, pay later society, but that is precisely how he inculcated it to us thousands of years ago. Living a life in moderation is like an extra dose of antibodies against financial diseases.

Then again, Chinese millennials are far more prone to the modern way of life, racking up debts as if money were raining down on them (often from their parents and grandparents). But that is a reflection for a separate subject.

CHAPTER FORTY-FIVE

DUE TO THE ECONOMIC downturn, I was once again searching for purpose. Even though Research Triangle Park had long established itself as one of the best places to live in the country, in my case it was not favorable for starting a business. North Carolina lacked the specific lures that northern New Jersey had by being close to the major metropolis that embodied business-minded communities, world-trade seaport, and rivers of foot-traffic. As a result, my international trade firm was self-sustainable at best, but had no potential to grow. I needed to change course and look for my next big thing, again.

In the early 1990s, the most revolutionary development was personal computers, led by the Windows 3.1x release in 1992. I decided to plunge right into this enormous pond, even though I knew it was my weak link—possibly my weakest. I had tried taking computer courses twice at U.C.—and dropped them twice. Those were the only times I ever dropped a course.

"Mountain does not move, so water has to turn." This Chinese saying draws a vivid picture of first-generation immigrants in America, especially the first wave of us in the early 1980s from Mainland China. We often must "trim our feet to fit the shoes."

Second-generation immigrants, including our daughter, are just the opposite. They often suffer from what behavioral science calls 'choice paralysis': it becomes much harder to make up one's mind when people are faced with too many options. But be it by fate or personality, I have never had this problem.

I set my business on autopilot. I then paid $3,000 for a six-month program to learn computer network management; it was the most I had ever spent on learning anything. After three months, IBM, the global tech company, hired me as a network consultant.

To start, they had to supply me with a long cheat sheet to show me how to answer questions when customers called. Nevertheless, I got my proverbial foot in the door, catching the perfect wave of the third industrial revolution. I rode this revolutionary tidal surge learning by doing.

Two years later, I jumped ship to work in a more refined environment at a major telecom company. The company's motto of self-management contrasted sharply with IBM's micro-management style, which was a major draw for me. And yet, as I soon found out, my position allowed little room for self-cultivation.

Ideas bubbled in my head. How could I break free from this feeling of treading on a nine to five hamster wheel? The glimmer of my ideas was met with a splash of cold water.

One day, strolling down the hallway after lunch, I ran into our executive director, Linda. "How are you doing, Cheng?" she asked cordially. Her eyes fixed on mine.

I had worked here for a year and a half now, and Linda would visit our team every once in a while to make announcements. Her bright and calm spirit would warm the room instantly. Each time she scanned the crowd, her eyes seemed to linger on me for a few seconds longer than others. It could have been my imagination, or it could be because mine was the only Chinese face in the 300-personnel Global Network Management Center (although many Chinese work in computer industries, most of them are software engineers). It made me feel like she already knew me well, even though we'd never had one-on-one time for anything until this moment.

I felt tense. "Hi, Linda...doing well. Thanks." I habitually paused, hoping for a proper English expression to come. Suddenly, I felt the need to say something, as though her soft and pleasant demeanor had injected me with an extra dose of courage. "I have been working on the same team for quite some time now...I think." I could not stop stuttering. "And it seems to me that I have learned almost everything I can by doing this same work. If I could work in a different environment, I might be able to learn new skills and have more potential to grow."

Linda waited patiently for me to finish my thought. "Let me think about it," she said.

A week passed. I had almost forgotten our encounter. Then one morning, the phone on my desk rang.

"Hey Cheng, I heard you wanted to do something new. You can come over and see me." It was the I.T. Director, Chip. We did not know each other personally.

My heart was pounding as if it were about to jump out of my chest. Needless to say, I reported to Chip's team the next day.

Chip, my new manager, was tall, with broad shoulders and bright eyes on a round face. He was always in a cheerful mood. He told me to research the industry, assess the new technologies, and then transcribe a report with my suggestions. The company's 'self-management' motto applied to me in a way I had never thought it could—to get paid to study the most innovative industry with no constraints.

Now my job had a new meaning. This switch was the most consequential turning point in my career, and even more so to my mindset. My Chinese look, error-filled English, noticeable accent, even my computer illiteracy—none were as much a career obstacle as I had led myself to believe. I learned to embrace all possibilities.

After that experience, I switched groups within the company two more times. I got to know more people and gained more skills. While I grew faster, Peiyuan and I cultivated our family's finances and pursued our hobbies.

Corporate America was like 'a heaven on earth' in the late 1990s. We were accustomed to spending money freely with corporate credit cards that had no limit, traveling for product-demos, or week-long training. One time, three of us went to Cleveland for the same meeting. We booked our flights separately, took out our own rental cars, and stayed in three different hotels. We only spoke together about where to find the best food in the city. No one seemed to notice anything wrong, especially management.

Doing my job did not feel like work; it always made me feel amazed and exhilarated. I was convinced that the stars had finally aligned in my favor.

CHAPTER FORTY-SIX

OF COURSE, NO PARTY lasts forever. The dotcom bubble burst in the early 2000s, and by the end of 2001, most technology-based stocks had crashed. This sudden change in tide caught everyone by surprise. The sharp economic downturn that followed the dotcom crash, plus the overspending to "prepare" for Y2K, had hit the markets hard. Then the 9/11 terror attacks in 2001 were the final blow that brought a decade's worth of growth to an end and propelled the world economy into a deep recession.

We felt it at our company as well. One day, our manager told us no one could travel. The next day, the free coffee, fruit drinks, and donuts all disappeared from the break room. A month later, the executive director, Linda, came to our team. "Our local security team is no longer needed. You should all start looking for another position internally within the next three weeks, or find employment elsewhere." She had never looked so serious. The entire company, once over 100,000 employees, shrank to less than 40,000 within a short period of time.

Sitting in front of my computer, I thought of someone in Florida, Jim. His team performed similar work to mine, but for the entire corporation. We had exchanged emails occasionally. I dialed Jim's number. "Jim, this is Cheng." He sounded like he remembered me, making me feel reassured. I went straight to the point. "Our team has been eliminated. If you need someone like me, I would be happy to work on your team."

Jim was the team leader; his five people were part of the CSO (Chief Security Office). "Actually, we could use people like you, Cheng, but we don't have an open position. No one in the CSO is hiring right now. But let me speak to my manager."

Although the call had gone well, a week passed, and I had all but forgotten about the conversation. Then my phone buzzed. "Hi Cheng, this is Gene. I am the manager of Jim's team." I did not recall having ever interacted with Gene, since he was in an upper management position. Nevertheless, his crisp voice put me on full alert.

"Jim told me that you are looking to transfer to his team, and yes, we need one more person to get a new project off the ground. However, it requires H.R.'s approval first, which is a tall order. As far as I know, no one can hire right now. But let me talk to my director and see if there is a way to work it out."

I thanked Gene. My hopes were now up. I started staring at the phone, longing for the miracle ring to sound again. But as another week passed with no word, hope dimmed a little more each day. Then the phone rang again.

"Cheng, I have good news for you." Gene's voice again! "I spoke to my director, who talked to his boss, all the way up to the V.P. The decision is finally clear. We can borrow a position to get you to work with Jim's team while awaiting a permanent position from H.R."

I could barely believe what I was hearing. I tried to listen carefully, all the while holding my breath.

"I know that Jim and his people are excited to have you. But when I asked them to tell me more, no one could say anything ... because none of them has ever met you." Gene sounded a little perplexed.

"Well, Gene, all I can say is…I will not let you down."

"I will start the paperwork for the transfer. Good luck, Cheng."

When I told my six team members, all Americans with formal technical degrees in computer engineering and more work experience than me, the exciting news, none of them had yet had an offer.

"How did you pull it off?" All eyes were on me.

"It started with a simple phone call two weeks ago," I said. "Beginner's luck?"

After reporting to my new team with the CSO, I worked from home full time. Since this was a development team responsible for our global network security, we were ranked one or two levels higher than local maintenance teams. Therefore, I was promoted to a senior position six months later, and then as a Principal Member of Tech Staff after another year.

All my friends from China and Cincinnati knew I'd never had formal computer training. They sometimes asked how I survived all the downsizings in the computer industry—even thrived—in my twenty plus years working for one company. I had no straight answer.

Although I had discovered a sense of purpose when I worked for Chip's team, it was my new manager, Gene, who had the most profound influence on me, one that went beyond work. Gene's leisure pursuit was acting in a Shakespeare company. People bought tickets to watch their shows during holidays and long weekends. His reverberating voice at our weekly meetings always resounded in my head. His carefully-chosen words were precise, even when writing a simple email, which prompted me to reread and consider them. Gene made me recognize the beauty and power of language, both at work and in everyday life.

"Each time you write something," Gene said during a one-on-one chat, "rewrite those sentences until all the words feel right to you." I have since applied that advice in all my writing, and as a result I have derived an enjoyment from words that indeed no words can describe.

In the end, my appearance, suspect technological background, self-developed skillset, or even my non-native language skills were not as important as people might suppose. So, perhaps my success at integration within the workplace, and within the culture on whole, had more to do with my good luck, almost as if an invisible and benevolent hand had been guiding me since my time in TianXi. Still, I have to wonder: do we, somehow, make our own luck? And if so, then how?

I do believe that we should trust our hearts—perhaps a little more than our brains—and try to connect with people without expecting anything in return. If we do so, we might just be amazed by what the future holds for us.

CHAPTER FORTY-SEVEN

ONCE OUR FAMILY HAD put down roots in North Carolina and our work-life became steadier, my birthplace and the people I grew up with started to resurface in my head. While my heart remained anchored in my mesmerizing new home, my identity was like a kite: flying high, but always with a string connecting it to its origin.

I traveled back to China for the first time in the late 1990s. However, the picture I saw when I arrived was a strange one, as if I had slipped into a place I had never been before. The culture shock of returning to my hometown was no less than the one I experienced in my one-way venture into America in the mid-1980s. All the buildings I was familiar with were either torn down or covered by enormous, commercial billboards. When I stood right in front of where our family had once lived in the "5.7 building," I could no longer connect it to my childhood.

All the first-floor doors of the building now opened onto the street, each now a shopfront, such as a restaurant, or a convenience store, or a massage salon. Endless small vendors lined the sidewalks selling all sorts of street food and daily essentials; and middle-aged men, looking dismal and confused, squatted behind baskets filled with cabbages or sweet potatoes.

I chatted with two of the men. They had the same story: their factory was closed, and they had nothing to do now. And they were all from the same Tiexi district in Shenyang. It had once been the base of China's most extensive heavy industry, famed for "the Cradle of the People's Republic." However, hundreds of factories had closed during the economic reform and restructuring of formally state-owned enterprises starting in the mid-1990s. One man, squatting behind a basket of eggs with a cigarette in hand told me how he had become a street vendor. One morning last month, he'd gone to work just the same as he had since he took over his father's position twenty years ago. A sizeable crowd was drawn to a sign near the entrance: *The steel factory will be closed tomorrow. All workers should see the human resource office to settle their compensation.*

When he was laid off, the man had received 10,000 yuan as his "buying-out-of-service" compensation. And that was it; no pension, no medical benefits, no social security income after twenty plus years of service. Since he had nothing else to do, he bought eggs from rural families and came to the city to resell them, making about twenty yuan a day as profit.

And there were 700,000 workers like him in my home city alone, being washed up by the wave of economic restructuring that had taken place over just a few years.

I met Xiao Wei, my young TianXi roommate, who carried a shiny beeper on his belt (a most trendy symbol at the time), and wore an edgy haircut. He had encountered the same fate, but used the compensation money to lease a small, rundown theater from the city (as part of the privatization process, the government started to lease out many money-losing public facilities to private citizens to run). Xiao Wei had divided the entire seating area into tiny cubicles, each big enough for two people, and showed old movies, as well as sold drinks and snacks in the lobby. It was nothing fancy, but the cubicle's cozy seating was enough to draw young people seeking privacy.

"I'm making ten times more now than punching the clock in my old factory," Xiao Wei said proudly, handing me a bottle of Coca-Cola (a rare and expensive drink at the time). He had turned himself into one of the earliest capitalists in Red China.

I still could not believe that Shenyang's industry center, once known as "the eldest son of the People's Republic of China," had now run its course. The next day, I took a taxi to the Tiexi District, looking for the factory I had briefly attended during the Cultural Revolution. It was the Shenyang Transformer Factory, which had employed 8,000 full-time workers in the old days.

The taxi driver happened to have worked in one of those district factories and had been laid off for the same reason. Now he drove a taxi, which was actually owned by someone else—two drivers for one car, twelve hours each shift, seven days a week. I told him I was looking for the Shenyang Transformer Factory.

"Consider yourself lucky if its front gates are still standing. Most likely, it's already been flattened by a bulldozer." He said it as if he were talking to someone from outer space.

It used to take forty minutes each way on a slow trolley to get to the factory. When the trolley was near Tiexi District, even when I was closing my eyes, the suffocating acrid stench would tell me I was getting close. The fetid air mixed with ingredients coming from smelters and chemical factories made it practically unbearable.

This time, as the taxi approached, I smelled nothing distinctive; all those high chimneys (some of them over 100 meters tall) were no longer in use. The air was breathable, and the sky looked blu*ish* now, rather than the yellow tint that I recalled.

The taxi stopped at a spacious plaza in front of a double-gated entrance, where two bulldozers were parked, ready to work. "Here you are!" The driver pointed to the gate.

The semicircular plaza and its double-gates were still familiar to me. Several fully-loaded shuttle buses would arrive every morning, and uniformed young men and women would flop out of the buses like fish pouring from a bucket. They were the happiest and proudest people during the Cultural Revolution—the pillars of the economy, with guaranteed salaries each month that were enough to support their families. They were the model class for everyone to look up to and learn from, as Mao advocated. As a middle-school boy in a work-to-learn program, I watched them arrive each morning for two months while I worked there, but somehow I had never envisioned myself becoming one of them for life. Now, though, it was eerily quiet. Inside the entrance weeds grew knee-high, even over the walkways. All the factory windows were either broken or dusty, a place fit only for ghosts.

"Ninety percent of the factories in Tiexi were ordered to shut down; only a few moved to suburban areas," the taxi driver told me. "Most were losing money anyway."

That trip left me with mixed feelings of nostalgia and melancholy. Shenyang, once a proud industry pillar of the country, was today the laggard of economic reform. It made me wonder: what would Daqing, the rural community I once cherished as a child, look like today?

I believe our actions always follow our thoughts. While on the phone with my mother one day, she told me that she'd learned that one of my childhood friends in Daqing, WanJiang, was working in Shenyang now. Some people in Daqing kept in contact with my mom through occasional phone calls and New Year greetings because she'd helped them one way or another in the past; and also because she was still well-informed about the village.

WanJiang had grown up in Daqing, but married a girl from Shenyang, so he lived in the city now. In the old days, I had always shared my cookies with him, and he often showed me where and when to pick the best seasonal fruits and vegetables to eat from the farm fields. I reconnected with WanJiang and expressed my interest in visiting Daqing during my next trip home. He gladly agreed to lead the way for me.

In early 2000, it took one and a half hours to get to Daqing from Shenyang via an air-conditioned tour bus on a newly-paved highway; whereas this same trip in the old days would have taken almost a day: first by train, then a bus, and lastly by horse-drawn wagon for the final two hours.

If WanJiang had not told me where to get off the bus, I would never have recognized it. Standing in the middle of the road about 100 yards from where our house used to be, I gazed around. My heart sank with a strong sense of melancholy. Looking at this same thoroughfare today, I saw no horses or donkeys drawing wagons, not even any chickens or ducks running along the roadside. And where had all the villagers gone? As far as my eyes could see, there were overgrown weeds by the roadside and on the rooftops of what had once been the General Store.

I walked around the village and through alleys full of loose bricks and muddy potholes: not much better than it had been four decades ago (although none of those had ever bothered me when I was ten). Along the way, WanJiang pointed to those places where our houses used to be, and where we had gone to the pond to skate in the winter and bathe in the summer. I missed the large cow-shed, from where Xiao Ren and I had herded a dozen or so cows to the fields for grazing.

At present I saw nothing that resembled any of these memories. As much as I understood that China had undergone many changes over the years, I had not expected to find what could only be described as a post-apocalyptic scene only a short drive away from a thriving city of eight million people. In fact, there is another side to China that those in the outside world, including most urban Chinese, don't see.

Dismayed by what I saw, I gave up reminiscing and asked WanJiang if we could find a few childhood friends still living there. In this 500-household village, everyone had known everyone else—except our family, who were the outsiders back then. WanJiang knocked on a few doors, and eventually we found two other elementary classmates. One was a girl who was a model student by any measure in those years: she was quiet, but often picked by teachers to answer questions; shy, but always ready to assist others with their homework; simply-dressed, but fit and spotless. She'd never left the village, and currently ran a food store so tiny it didn't have a storefront sign. It took us a while to find her store, even though we knew its name. She told us the sign had blown away and was never replaced.

"Everyone knows this store. Everyone knows me. So why bother to have a sign?" she said when I brought it up to break the ice. Conversation faltered as we stared at each other after going through what were now distant memories. Her glossy cheeks had darkened and wrinkled now.

Another gentleman, who was also from our class four decades before, was overjoyed to see me when WanJiang mentioned to him that I'd come from halfway around the world just to see Daqing and my childhood friends. However, I could not recall his name and felt too awkward to ask.

The four of us walked into the only restaurant in the village. We were the sole customers in the dining area. I then noticed that the "menu" was simply a display, like a produce stand in the marketplace. My eyes lit up when I spotted a huge water tank with live fish circling. Each fish weighed about four pounds, all from the lake a stone's throw away from the restaurant's back door. The female owner and chef greeted us. Her plump face burst into an amiable smile.

"What do you have for meals?" I asked.

"Anything you see on display," she readily replied.

"How do you cook the fish?" My eyes were locked on that tank.

"The way I always do." Obviously, she never felt the need to name any of the dishes, much less describe how she would cook them. I pointed to a few items on display and a fish, leaving the cook to work her magic.

I knew that there was no more authentic cooking than this: no recipes, no explanations, and the ingredients used changed from season to season (even from dish to dish) depending on what grew in the backyard and what was caught in the lake. Farm-to-table was not a new trend here; it had been—and still is—the only way people prepare food in this village.

I suddenly felt more at home, sensing the indigenous sincerity in the owner's tone that instantly took me back to the old days. The four of us sat around a table sipping tea, catching up on the four decades of experience that had somehow slipped away.

"Where are all the people now?" The question I'd stifled since the moment I stepped off the bus now burst out irrepressibly.

"All the young and able people have gone to the cities looking for work." The answer came out just as irrepressibly, if not more so, from the second gentleman. "I'm too sick to leave," he said, ending with a sigh. As he did so, he pulled up his shirt with one hand, exposing his abdomen. With a hypodermic needle in his other hand, he injected himself with insulin. "I was so excited to see you, I forgot to do this before eating." I did not know what to say.

"Nowadays, I need to take care of my mother; she has not gotten out of bed for a year, and she probably never will," the model student lamented, her eyes staring down in resignation: nothing like when she'd confidently answered the teacher's questions in class in the old days.

"And why are the road conditions so bad?" I asked.

"We simply can't afford to pave all the roads, even if the government promises to pay half the cost," The former model student revealed. "Anyway, this place is my home, and it has everything I need." Sensing more questions, she added: "Life is easy here."

We still had touched only half the fish. The owner simply had cooked too much food, and yet the meal had cost the equivalent of fifteen dollars for the four of us, including beer and rice wine, and I came to understand the meaning of "Life is easy here."

When evening fell, I was on the bus back to Shenyang. Skyscrapers illuminated the panorama as they rose against the distant horizon. It was as if I had time-travelled to a prehistoric world, only to return to a contemporary one. Suddenly, I realized that the gleaming parts of China, the miracle that the world now recognized, had mostly been built by workers from the countryside. Officially, they had no social status in the cities where they worked because of the Hukou system. Most of them lived crowded into modular or prefab houses near construction sites, often dubbed "ant dwellings." They could not fairly share in the "reform dividends," such as medical care, well-paid employment, and education for their children, which the urban residents now took for granted.

Data from the China National Bureau of Statistics shows the total number of migrant workers in 2017 reached 286.52 million—one-fifth of the population. They made an average monthly income of 3,485 yuan (the equivalent of 500 U.S. dollars), on which they must support themselves as well as the families they left behind in the countryside, usually their children and aging parents too. Based on research, half the population in China is left behind in the fast-growing economy because of the Hukou and land system in China.

Behind the spectacular scenes in China are the hundreds of millions of people who have given up their family lives to create better ones for urban residents. These migrant workers work on iPhone assembly lines, construction sites, or wait tables in the restaurants. They are still doing it today while going through hardships far beyond what most people imagine.

Whenever a book or an article I read mentions anything about the "Rust Belt States" in the Northern U.S., once known for steel production, it always leads me to think with a heavy heart of Shenyang and the three provinces in northern China. These vast areas all fit the definition of "Rust Belt" in America today; they even parallel each other geometrically.

The Chinese version of the "Rust Belt" was a consequence of the drastic shift in government policy in 1996: to stop guaranteeing jobs for anyone who worked in the money-losing factories so that those factories could either achieve a turnaround or close. It was another milestone in progress—upsetting many, shocking most, but liberating the minds of everyone toward the market economy.

The economic reform led to another new but common scene: outsized crowds on the corners of major streets with 'For Hire' signs in hand. They were laid-off factory workers, handymen, housekeepers, and college students, all ready to work by the hour, the day, the month, or, for the lucky few, even longer. The signs of a market economy were like spring bamboo shoots sprouting all over the country. The dramatic reforms had unleashed remarkable gains through increased efficiency and competition, but at the expense and severe pain endured by hundreds of millions of people.

Competing for jobs fostered its own competition in schools. All the young people in middle and high schools had a much different school life than what I had experienced. My brother's daughter was in high school at the time. Every time we went out to eat, she would bring her schoolbag with her. She would do her schoolwork for the twenty minutes before the food was served and then again after eating. A dozen people sat around the dinner table, yet no one appeared surprised—except me.

When I was her age, I rarely brought a schoolbag even to school. Deep down, I felt that the fortuitous circumstances had suited me well, not spending my upbringing years on passing tests. In my mind, all these "one question, one solution" testing models did more harm to a young brain than good. The "pressure cooker" learning environment sucked the life out of them, leaving no time or energy for free-thinking, imagination, or even fun.

Over the years, I've become more convinced that society is the best school (Mao might be partially right for advocating that idea, although not with the same intent). As my favorite writer, William Zinsser, puts it, "learning is a tonic;" at least, for those who want to learn. Thus, they never stop doing it. For those under pressure to learn, they are more likely to stop learning after passing each test, especially once the first paycheck hits their bank account.

Quite a substantial and noteworthy list of household names in American business, and now in Chinese business and culture, too, have famously broken away from top colleges to pursue their passion and visions. Steve Jobs. Larry Ellison. Bill Gates. In China, Jack Ma became interested in the English language as a young boy, and during his teens worked as a guide for foreign tourists to Hangzhou. Ma failed the entrance exam for the Hangzhou Teachers College twice. He was admitted on the third try, in 1984, and he graduated with a bachelor's degree in English in 1988. These entrepreneurs are the ones creating real-life success on a scale far beyond academic predictions.

So I ask: Why isn't learning encouraged as a labor of love instead of the unending and pointless motion spent on the treadmill of formal education?

CHAPTER FORTY-EIGHT

AFTER MY FIRST TRIP back to China, I went back every year to see my aging parents and to keep up with the changes there: a task which I found to be virtually impossible, even for a homegrown boy like me. Aside from the constant cosmetic surgery that made my hometown completely unrecognizable, it was the inner changes of the people that struck me the most. With economic growth being on an upward spiral for many years, as soon as urban young couples have steady jobs, their children's futures become their top priority. The traditional obsessive form of parenting has become ever more manifest. But how far are today's young parents willing to go?

One close college friend had a daughter who had just had her first child. "Wang Shushu (uncle in Chinese), what is the easiest way to emigrate to North America?" the daughter asked me shortly after I met their family in Shenyang. "We would like our son to have a Western education." That child was only one year old. These parents are far from alone in major Chinese cities today.

An official Chinese *Xinhua News* story revealed that a family spent more than $200,000 USD to buy a forty-square-foot apartment in Beijing's best school district. The apartment was too small to be habitable, but it was a sure ticket for their child to attend a top-ranked school. Another survey showed that almost half of wealthy Chinese plan to move abroad within five years, and America was one of the top destinations. Their very first reason was for their children's education.

The flight from Shanghai to Chicago is fourteen hours: that long in one seat makes it a perfect time to hear the most intimate personal stories from strangers from anywhere in the world. After two hours in the boundless blue sky, my attention was drawn to the couple beside me: they were in their early forties, the wife near the window and her husband in the middle seat. Their eyes were scintillating with excitement. I was reading, as usual, and the English novel in my hands might have intrigued the husband. When I folded the book to rest my eyes, he broke the silence.

"Do you speak Chinese?" he asked in English.

"Yes," I replied in perfect Chinese, "are you traveling for sightseeing?"

"To do research, so we can make an important decision for our family," the wife interjected. Her clear words were like water gushing from a lifted gate.

"This is our first trip to America. We are going to Charlotte, North Carolina, where we have friends, to visit three elementary schools and see which one is more suitable for our son." She said it all in one breath and dipped her head to me.

She told me that their son was ten, an excellent swimmer in his school, but not happy with the primary curriculum. They were convinced the Chinese educational system would suffocate their boy's ingenuity in a sea of textbooks, whereas American schools would inspire independent thinking and cultivate individuality. After reaching middle-income status in a major city in China, their top concern was their only son's future, so they had made this decision, although not without sacrifices.

"We have done a lot of research and prefer American education," the wife continued while the husband nodded in agreement. "I will live with my son in the U.S., learning English and teaching music part-time, while my husband works in China and comes to see us sometimes." They obviously had a clear picture of what their family life in America would be, even though their feet had yet to touch American soil.

"For us, it may be hard, but worth it." Her words spoke of confidence. "Oh, by the way, how would we best ship a cello from China to the U.S.?"

They both meant business, I could tell. While I admired their quixotic determination, the images of typical new immigrant life flashed through my head: a single mom raising a ten-year-old boy in an unfamiliar neighborhood, speaking little English, teaching cello, plus handling chores year-round...

"Your visa status for accompanying your school-aged son would not permit you to work in the U.S.," I pointed out one of the most obvious issues off the top of my head. "And the healthcare expenses will seem astronomical: you should be prepared for that. Plus, the ongoing quarrels between the leaders of the two countries could potentially derail immigration plans for years..." I paused, as the glow on their faces dimmed.

After a time, words trickled out from the wife in a far less enthusiastic tone. "Well, all my friends already know about our decision. Or perhaps we should wait for a couple of years?"

"Our son has told all his friends, and he really couldn't wait to go to America..." The husband muttered back to her.

"What beverage would you like?" Food service broke the unease and then left us in the perpetual humming quiet, putting me in a very awkward situation. I worried I might have said too much and possibly ruined their trip.

Nevertheless, most Chinese parents stick doggedly to "obsessive parenting" as a reflection of their high expectations for their children. Possibly because of that, few of these kids can reach an elite level in any field in America (far less than Indian immigrants in the U.S., to put it into perspective).

It is not hard to understand that successful human beings are unlikely to be raised in an autocratic educational system or an overbearing parental environment; they must grow up in a self-driven and passion-oriented culture.

I'm reminded of a question I once encountered that went viral online: "Why can't China, a country that has a population over 1.4 billion, create one person like Steve Jobs?" The obvious answer is that people like Steve Jobs cannot be "created": they are self-made.

CHAPTER FORTY-NINE

As ONE WHO HAS now crisscrossed the Pacific for decades, I often wonder what one thing can empirically distinguish people on one side of the ocean from people on the other side?

Food culture is the most obvious aspect that comes to mind. But that is superficial, and only a matter of preference. Yet, deep down, the way we eat, especially our (mis)perceptions of different types of food, can subconsciously give away our true national and cultural identities.

Another time when I was on a flight back to the U.S., seated by my side was a man in his late forties. He introduced himself as having been a policeman for twenty years in Shanghai. His daughter attended Johns Hopkins University as an undergraduate student; this was his fifth time visiting her.

"What is your impression of America?" I asked him.

After a pause, he said, "In Shanghai, no policeman carries a gun during their regular duties. By comparison, they have armed all the policemen in New York to the teeth."

A professional observation, indeed! I had never noticed it, even though I traveled to Shanghai every year. How blind our eyes can be!

"How about American people that you have met?" I grew more curious now.

"The people I know through my daughter seem to be very stingy," he said after a little more thought. "Every time we go out to eat, if I invite them, I normally order at least six to eight different dishes. But when they invite me, it is normally one plate for each person, with one piece of steak, cornbread, and some minor things on the side." The policeman sounded a little irritated.

"Chicken pasta or sandwich?" A flight attendant interrupted our conversation to serve lunch.

"What did she just say?" The policeman asked me to translate it into Chinese.

Once I told him about the two meal choices, he frowned. In his mind, I could tell, anything other than authentic Chinese food was a major cultural barrier.

While Jewish homes have two sets of dishes, two dishwashers, and two sinks in one kitchen (one set for dairy products and another that remains Kosher), well-off Chinese families often have two full kitchens. The closed one (no guests should see the inside) is dedicated to cooking Chinese food to satisfy the scrupulous appetite, while the open, embellished one is for boiling soup or water, mostly as a stylistic statement.

By that comparison, it is not an overstatement to say that food, or the way people indulge in food, has been the longest-running stream of collective lore for the Chinese.

"China is too old, too diverse; it's too deep and complex," one of my American friends once griped. "I've spent decades exploring it, but still feel ignorant."

I agree. Even in reading about China every day, one might still only succeed in skimming the surface. I suggested that my American friend get to know more about Chinese food first, especially the underlying meaning of food for the Chinese people. Follow the vine to find the root.

In Analects, a disciple asked Confucius, "How to govern a state?" Confucius replied, "Only sticking to three rules would do: military, food, and people's loyalty."

In Chinese history, famines caused by either natural disasters or political upheavals (although never a religious war) triggered countless uprisings, which often led to the end of one dynasty or another. Mao Zedong founded New China with the same strategy, followed by famished, landless peasants who followed him to fight rather than starve.

"People regard food as heaven," is a well-known axiom that emphasizes how vital food has been throughout history. Current Chinese leaders, with no exception, place stability as the foremost priority. That means having enough food on the table for 1.4 billion in a country where half of them still live in a subpar standard.

The same phrase, "people regard food as heaven," has a different meaning for Chinese Americans. It is all about food qualities and authenticity—not all Chinese foods are created equal.

Most Americans can name quite a few well-known cooking styles like Sichuan, Cantonese, or Peking duck. But for those who like to experiment, one should ask a waitress if they have a separate menu for the Chinese. Be prepared for things like steamed whole fish, unpeeled shrimp, chicken feet, pork belly with skin on, and pork intestines. And that is only the starting point.

Foreign visitors to China quickly notice the importance of evening dinners—twenty plates piled high on a rotating tray is not an uncommon sight. The atmosphere often reflects how things have gone during the day. Sometimes, the most critical issues get worked out right there, after a few rounds of baijiu. Coming to dinner prepared with what to say and what to skip is an art within the culture.

Then again, the question of tea versus coffee is like drawing a line in the sand, splitting the two cultures as clearly as the Pacific Ocean.

Starbucks Coffee has become one of the most successful American brands in China. Yet, after over two decades of Starbucks shops in this Eastern land, Chinese consumers drink only five cups of coffee per year according to the International Coffee Organization. In comparison, my American friend and doubles tennis partner, Rick, consumes more than that in one morning.

I drink three cups of coffee every morning and then tea later in the day. Every time Rick and I carpool to tennis in the morning, his coffee mug makes me feel like I am still only halfway through assimilation in America.

But for people in China, even as habit-forming as coffee is, adding it to their routine shopping list will take several generations, if ever. Similarly, Rick would never start his day with tea. This exhibits how difficult it is to make even one simplistic change in culture.

However, over decades of culture-crossings, one of the most gratifying progressions for me is to fully appreciate both coffee and tea, and to savor beef tenderloin and braised pork just the same. And thanks to cultural globalization, I do not need to cross the ocean, or even leave town, to do any of these things.

CHAPTER FIFTY

IF AUTHENTIC INDIGENOUS FOOD introduces people to a new social standard, then distinctive drinking customs would lead them further into a new culture.

For thousands of years, the ocean and Himalayas have blocked the exchange of drinking cultures between the East and the West, among many other rituals. Until now, baijiu or "white liquor" is nowhere to be found in American stores. Therefore, the code needed for Americans to appreciate baijiu is still waiting to be cracked.

China's baijiu is made from grain, running between fifty to sixty percent ABV. As an aficionado of both baijiu and red wine, I believe that both Americans and Chinese can understand—and even learn to savor—each other's rich drinking customs alongside their own.

My appreciation for baijiu started with my father's daily ritual when I was in middle school. He would put a small bottle of baijiu in a dish of boiled water to warm it before supper (there was no underage drinking regulation in China until 2006). The room would instantly fill with a distinctive, opulent aroma that would draw me out from my room. My father often let me sip a little, and I enjoyed it tremendously. Day by day, I became more enamored with it.

Baijiu is potent, and fiery, creating warmth throughout the body. Like wine, baijiu has many brands and flavors, and is produced in various parts of China with prices ranging from $10 to over $300 for a 500ml bottle. But unlike wine, it pairs with almost any warm meal impeccably well, producing the same ecstatic effect on discerning palates.

Another deciding element, and my favorite, is whom you drink it with. "A thousand glasses is inadequate when baijiu meets an understanding soul." This famous Chinese saying sets the tone perfectly.

The drinking customs in China place a lot of emphasis on social functions. For foreign visitors, a well-selected bottle for dinner with the locals often reveals how well the day has gone, and whether it is for business or leisure. The spirit of the gathering brings out camaraderie and social bonding.

On formal occasions, the rules are implicit. The host usually raises his cup first, and guests follow, raising theirs slightly lower to clink cups with the host or someone with higher social status. Whether the host drinks half a cup or bottoms up, the guests will follow suit.

If you want to make a toast, saying "Ganbei" is the closest to "Cheers" in Chinese; however, its direct translation is to finish one's drink or "bottoms up." Some local people might take it that way, so be ready for that.

Mao Zedong served Moutai (the most renowned brand of baijiu) at state dinners during Richard Nixon's historical visit to China in the early '70s. Henry Kissinger once commented to Deng Xiaoping during their meeting years later, "If we drink enough Moutai, we can solve anything."

Can baijiu still work its wonder in resolving our differences today? This, I believe, holds true anytime and anywhere, if only people are willing to try it.

CHAPTER FIFTY-ONE

WHILE NURTURING NEW HOBBIES, I noticed I had a knack for untangling financial knots. It is a goal I had not deliberately pursued, but my lucky car-purchasing and house hunting experiences, plus years of family financial management, are solid testimony. It could be credited to Confucius's influence, my Hakka genes, the re-education I received in TianXi, or perhaps my five-plus years of schooling in Western economics.

Besides the Doctrine of the Mean running through my veins, I am a decades-long reader of the *Wall Street Journal*, becoming the last dinosaur in the neighborhood that goes out to fetch the morning paper. However, it is not the analysts' speculations that pique my interest, but the act of feeling the pulse of the financial and economic well-being of the world. All these readings have subconsciously imbued me with a distinctive perspective that steers me to act when the time feels right.

I believe "less is more" and "patience is a virtue" in financial management. I put my faith—with a meaningful chunk of my wealth—in the best visionaries on earth. Time is another open secret. Stocks, mutual funds, annuities, real estate, and bonds, plus my pension and 401K, all confer the benefit of compounding through time. With patience, most of the financial trees I have planted have borne fruit, including the acquisition of a home in Shanghai, which killed two birds with one stone: a foothold in China's best city and long-term investment in financial and lifestyle diversity.

Shanghai has become another city we can call home. Peiyuan and I are China "green card" holders, officially marking us as permanent residents in China (how times have changed since we received our American green cards three decades ago!). China's Permanent

Residence cards happen to be one of the hardest in the world to obtain since they were first issued in 2004. For example, according to an Annual Report on Chinese International Migration, only 1,576 Chinese green cards were issued in 2016. In comparison, in 2016 alone, the U.S. issued 1.18 million green cards, according to the United States Department of Homeland Security.

In 2003, I bought an apartment for my mom in Shenyang, which gives me a real sense of homecoming every time I see her. We now have three places we can rightly call home, which calls to mind another Chinese saying, "A clever rabbit always has three nests."

Deep down, I have found that these three homes carry different meanings for me: emotionally, geographically, or culturally. Shenyang, undoubtedly, is the place I hold dearest to my heart. My childhood friends there have lived in that one place their entire lives, but never seem bothered by people, like me, from the outside who hold different political or sociological views. Somehow, they settle me and keep my feet on the ground whenever we meet. Through them, I see life can be uncomplicated, easygoing, and blissful.

In Shenyang, my mom has always been the anchor for our family. At the age of ninety-three, she remembers more than two dozen of her living relatives, how they are all related, and their childhood stories in Zhencheng Lou. She is the oldest of her extended family now, and the most respected among them.

In Chinese tradition, the New Year's greetings start on Chinese New Year's Day. So, every year during that day, after finishing her breakfast, she sits by the phone to answer all the New Year's greetings she receives, which takes more than half the day. I sometimes have to dial five times to get through to her. Therefore, New Year's Day is her happiest day of the year.

What's more, some of her former students, all now around eighty years old themselves, bring her comfort and pride. They come to see her a few times each year (during National Teacher's Day, Christmas Day, and her birthday). I can tell that it is her students, once the 'Red Guards' in the old days—far more than any official acknowledgment or words I could say—that have helped heal her emotional wounds inflicted in the Cultural Revolution.

Our newest home, Shanghai, feels like an in-between place, both literally (I always take a direct flight to land in Shanghai before going to Shenyang) and culturally. Known as the "Paris of the East" in the 1930s, Shanghai has since kept up its reputation.

Shanghai means 'upper sea' in Chinese, and its motto is to "act like the sea that is inclusive of all rivers." According to 2019 surveys, Shanghai accommodates the largest expat population in China: more than 200,000. Anyone who lives in Shanghai would notice that even most local people hardly speak Shanghai dialects in public anymore (either Mandarin or even English will do). Among hundreds of cable TV channels, you would find more that are English-speaking than Shanghai dialects. In restaurants, Westerners eat, drink, and laugh at each other's jokes, which makes me feel more like a foreigner sometimes.

Lastly, our North Carolina home is where our family spends the most time together, including our truly adorable granddaughter that Cintty has brought into the world. This place is where my imagination is boundless, allowing me to grow beyond my innate geo-boundaries.

I often hear of people who lack a sense of identity and belonging, and are thus less willing to step out of their own comfort zone. And I often experience people misidentifying me when we first meet—like the young couple on my flight who had to ask if I could speak Chinese. But somehow, I don't feel confused about who I am, not because I am so certain of myself, but because I feel comfortable with the people around me.

I like to meet with my childhood friends in Shenyang, even though they have not earned a college degree, much less set foot outside their home turf. They never treat me as an outsider simply because we eat at the same food joint, drink the same beers, and laugh in the way with which we are all familiar.

Among Americans, I do not feel out of place, either. Once I open up, most are genuinely curious to learn about my life's journey. To them, someone starting a new life in a foreign country with only 200 dollars is almost beyond comprehension. Who said that East and West could never meet? In me, it would seem that the two cultures complement each other perfectly.

Adaptation theory states that organisms adjust to their environment in order to improve their chances of survival within that environment. In retrospect, this theory might explain why I took such a different path than most Chinese people: this was my way to survive and then be able to flourish in various types of soils through adaptations. By navigating the road less traveled, I have found that there is a far more diverse and magnificent culture outside one's own innate and self-preserving boundaries.

Over the last two decades of rising through the corporate ranks, my experience has been both financially and intellectually rewarding; but only to a point, because my virtual office always followed me, even halfway around the world, stylishly packed into an iPhone and conveniently tucked into my pocket. Now, being fortunate enough to conclude the professional chapter of my life, I have realized that time to myself is a pleasure to be experienced without guilt because it allows me to wander and explore without a pre-defined destination.

Chapter Fifty-two

"Many people go fishing all of their lives without knowing that it is not fish they are after." The wit of Henry Thoreau crossed my mind one day when my eyes fell upon my twenty-five-year-old tennis racquet hanging on the wall. After falling in love with the game over two decades earlier, I have awakened to the fact that, for me, playing tennis can be likened to fishing in that regard.

Growing up playing ping pong, tennis had never entered my dreams. Ping pong was in my veins, but tennis looked more like a proper game. I seemed to encounter tennis courts—all well-groomed, lighted, and free to use—more often than convenience stores in my North Carolina town. Along with used tennis balls that I collected around the courts, the Wilson Hammer 4.0 that I now keep on my wall was what got me started.

In years past, I practiced against the wall, training my footwork and mimicking the pros I saw on T.V.; then, it was off to the real courts. Before I knew it, my name was on the list of 100-plus Saturday morning players. I then joined Kildaire Farms Racquet and Swim Club and a USTA League—to this day I am the only Chinese face. The nicknames I earned ('Backboard' and 'Chengerator') make me feel like I am not an easy match on court.

It did not take me long to fit right into our sizeable local tennis community. Our team played locally and traveled to meet out-of-town players or to attend the State Championships during the tournament season. We carpooled together, guzzled beers, trash-talked, and genuinely cared about one another.

Thanks to tennis, I met Rick, who has been a savvy tennis enthusiast since his high school days. Thenceforth, he and I have played as tennis doubles ever since. Any time we both show up at court, we are recognized as the only *de facto* doubles partners—locally or at USTA State Championships matches—over the last two decades.

Coincidentally, we are the same age. Rick loves classic American literature. He is married to a Chinese girl, Cathy, who publishes a Chinese newspaper (although Rick can't speak more than five Chinese words as far as I can tell). Off the court, with craft brews on the table, we often geek out on any number of topics well into the wee hours (often until Cathy calls). It is not like we do not have our differences, but we have both learned to leave our assumptions (cultural, political, and personal) at home. We see each other for who we are, not what we are expected to be.

Naturally, Rick becomes the first American reader and commentator of my writings, including this book. Besides tennis, our next episode will be backpacking and town-hopping along the Mediterranean coast.

Norman, the captain of our USTA League team, organizes matches for our team several times a week and always brings extra beer for others. In our club, which has over 375 members, he appears to know everything about every player: their whereabouts if they don't show up, their physical well-being, and so forth. When Norman knew I had an elbow issue, he brought me his new, elbow-friendly tennis racquet for me to use. He would ask how I was doing if he did not see or hear from me for more than a week. Every team needs someone like Norman to hold a large community together, and for us, Norman fits that role. He is the influence that encourages me to treat tennis as a culturally bonding experience.

I often wondered why I was the only Mainland Chinese for more than two decades to settle in this melting pot community. How could I nudge my countrymen to come out of their comfort zone? When I was invited to be on the USTA North Carolina Growth Leagues Committee, I saw it as an opportunity to better promote the game—and the culture—in Asian communities.

"Most Asian players I know play tennis more frequently than I do," I said during our annual retreat in Pinehurst Resort, North Carolina, "but for some reason they play only among themselves. As a personal goal, I want to try to change that."

I co-hosted a tennis tournament with the Chinese American Friendship Association (which is comprised of over 1,000 Chinese members in the RTP region of North Carolina). We invited people from all races in the nearby counties to participate. The intention (for me, at least) was to open a door for everyone to play with people they had never met before. As it turned out, the event was a blast for everyone. In the end, we formed a tennis committee and decided to make it an annual cultural event.

Socially, the impact of tennis on me has grown far beyond a sport. Sometimes, when a hot-button issue strikes a nerve, discussions can become heated in this large tennis community, which is made up of people from all walks of life. One of those topics was about the repeal of a statute by the State legislature to safeguard sexual orientation. The topic included subjects such as homosexuality, pedophilia, incest, and bestiality. During the discussion, some remarks seemed to put homosexuality and pedophilia in the same category. As one might imagine among more than 100 people, there were as many opinions as there were throughout America. In China, people mostly kept their opinions on such subjects to themselves. Not so in America; and such discussions really got my mind churning. In front of me an ancient, reserved culture was contrasted with the youngest, most diverse one. It was like examining day and night at the same time. But once I gathered my thoughts, another voice entered: "Labels are for filing. Labels are for clothing. Labels are not for people." This affirmation from Tennis Hall of Famer Martina Navratilova resonated deeply with me.

Why do people often fall for labels (social, political, or otherwise) as a substitute for critical thinking? Just as with my earliest musings on the various "isms," I wondered: do all these short-hand names actually inform or distort the truth?

For example, how wearing a protective face mask during a pandemic has become yet another socio-political rallying point is beyond me. It reminds me of the colors we knew we should—and definitely should not—wear during the Cultural Revolution to display our political stance. The dull gray or blue suits in Mao-style or soldier's pine-green were the most "correct" ideological statement, while wearing bright colors was tempting fate. That might sound bizarre, but that was China during the 1960s and early 1970s, when the country was a completely closed one—both physically and mentally.

Nevertheless, such musings, born of my favorite physical pastime, have made me realize that while striving for an intellectual mind and an athletic body separately, I have arrived at a whole that is greater than the parts. This can best be described as crossing a cultural bridge. I would have remained a social and emotional outsider without cultural integration. It is an acculturating process. And tennis has played an essential part in that process.

Nothing is accidental. Over the years, my worldview has evolved in many ways: my tea ritual easing into one of coffee, baijiu swapped out for wine, our vegetable garden converted into a grassy lawn, a stir-fry wok side-by-side with a grill, and, more particularly, Confucian ideals melding into Christian theology. This is a cultural transformation: a conforming proletariat metamorphosed into an individualist. Or my personal version of *How the Steel Is Tempered.*

EPILOGUE

- - - - - - - - - - - - - - - - - - - -

"TURNING SIXTY, ONE HAS developed placid ears." At that age, according to Confucius, one has seen through the world, and is thus not easily irked by the words of others.

One night, however, I was jolted out of sleep by a sobering realization. For a long while, I lay in bed wondering—like a spendthrift recalling where all his money has gone—what had become of all the time that had once belonged only to me? I started compiling an inventory of recent developments that seemed to steal time away from me. And I soon realized that a big change was in store for me.

Upon turning sixty, I said farewell to my coworkers and corporate life; and once liberated from the work world I had known for many years, I signed up for a three-day writer's workshop at Ossabaw Island, Georgia, marking the end of one long trek and the start of another.

On a private boat to Ossabaw Island (the only method of getting there), I met a couple in their early fifties. Curious as to why they were joining this workshop, I learned that the man had authored thirty-six novels. "Wow!" I said, "I haven't even read thirty-six English novels."

After settling in my room, and before the welcome dinner, I went out to look around the restored 1880s hunting lodge, the only construction nestled in the wood on a solitary island. A middle-aged man with a guitar in his hand sat on the front porch.

"Hi, Cheng," he said before I'd even introduced myself to him, "I'm Tony." We had already exchanged a few emails. Tony was the Ossabaw Island Writers' Retreat Director and a prize-winning author, Tony Ray Morris.

As the only Chinese face on the island, it was as if my name was written on my forehead. I also felt I had contacted him at the time of applying for the retreat, and he'd wanted to read some of my writing to make sure this retreat would be right for me. We shook hands like two long-time friends running into each other again.

We then chatted about writing in general, and specifically about my writing conundrum. The problem was that I knew I loved writing more than anything else, but I also faced enormous obstacles. Tony told me all these obstacles could be overcome with time and suggested that I write a book about my personal experience.

"Who would want to read about me or my life?" I thought he must be kidding.

"If Amy Tan can write a book about herself..." Tony looked serious.

In my mind, there was no way I could write a book that people would want to read. And yet, Tony had sown the first seed within me, which then remained dormant for a few years. Looking back, that brief conversation with Tony Morris was no less than a transcendent moment.

Returning from that workshop, and mingling with aspiring and accomplished writers, editors, and presenters—people that I might have otherwise never met—I felt like a changed man. A new ritual emerged for me: devoting the first three hours each morning to filling blank pages. I created a blog entitled, *A Man of a Certain Age on the Road*. While journeying, my diasporic nature let my eyes and ears absorb sights, sounds, smells, and folk stories—from my birth country and from my adopted country.

Karen, our community magazine editor, invited me to join her and a few others for a local food review. I ended up authoring eight articles within one year, including reviews on Ethiopian, Irish, and Lebanese food. These exotic foods are all within a fifteen-minute drive from my home, but I had never known of their existence. I have since learned that Ethiopia is coffee's birthplace, and the way that they treat coffee makes Starbucks look like an amateur. Guinness Draught is an Irish brand (not British, as I thought). And Lebanese food is an infusion of French, Arabian, and Mediterranean styles, becoming their own deep-rooted culinary tradition.

During our gatherings, Karen introduced me as a writer, a title which had never crossed my mind before. One year later, Karen told me she had gone back to teaching for financial reasons. I have missed her—her sincere way of nurturing and nudging—ever since.

I joined the Western Wake Human Health and Service Advisory Committee before my retirement. Our bi-weekly meetings focus on helping single moms, children from broken homes, and jobless and families in need. My desire to contribute had originated during our days in Cincinnati. After we came home from the hospital with our newborn daughter, a large container had appeared outside our apartment each morning before 6:00 am (I never met the delivery person). In the box was always a gallon of milk, eggs, cheese, and other food. As it turned out, the hospital system considered us, as students, automatically qualified for benefits from the Department of Human Service and Health for six months!

Now it is my chance to honor my debt from several decades ago. The Advisory Committee Director, another Karen, also introduced me as a writer, and that lit my eyes far more than my title of Principal Member of Tech Staff at work ever had. I have no idea how she knew, because I never sent any of my writing to her. And back then, I hardly even realized it myself.

Since then, I have signed up for a Mentoring Program for new international students called the Global Training Initiative, which is hosted by North Carolina State University. At our first meeting I introduced myself as having been one of those students, although that was thirty-five years ago at the University of Cincinnati. Truly, I wish there had been such a program when I landed in a strange land as a foreign student.

A week later, the Program Director, Randy, arranged for me to meet my student mentee. Shiren, a twenty-two-year-old graduate student, had come to the U.S. two months earlier from Beijing and enrolled in a two-year master's program with a major in statistics.

Shiren and I first met in a café near the N.C. State campus. His pale face and shy eyes appeared tense, but I saw a notably focused and driven young man. Looking at him, I seemed to be meeting my younger self.

"How do I get an internship position while a graduate student?" After a brief introduction, he asked me this question, possibly the only one he had for me.

"Maybe we should get our priorities straight first," I replied. "Once you prepare yourself well, this and many other things you want will come along before you know it." I was trying to make him look a little farther down the road than his immediate concern.

"Your first homework," I said before our meeting was over, "is to prepare your personal story, and tell me about it, in English, when we meet again." I emphasized that he should spend some time on it, to force more of his personality into it each time he practiced the story by himself, so that it was more than a pure event report.

"Every time you meet a new professor or someone in the cafeteria, or an interviewer for a job, imagine that each one is eager to get to know you. An engaging personal story will invite others into your life." While conveying my thoughts to the young man, I felt I could have been talking to my younger self.

After our initial meeting, every time we met we swapped personal stories for the first thirty minutes. The young student's narratives became more illustrative, infused with his distinct family background and personal flair. Soon, his eyes displayed confidence.

Yet, I have learned more from him than the other way around, almost as if I were going through a reverse mentorship program. He is younger and less experienced, but far more immersed in social media, technology and other unfamiliar cultural manifestations that I need to catch up on in this digital age.

New technologies become obsolete quickly nowadays, but old-fashioned storytelling will never be outdated. Instead, it can be a way to make a good and lasting first impression when you meet someone.

A few months later, Shiren told me that he had received a job offer that he'd wanted very much but never thought he could have gotten. By that time, I had a new student mentee assigned to me, but I had a special feeling of happiness for my first mentee.

Having weathered the longest and the worst political hailstorm in modern Chinese history, I have developed my own ideological hang-ups, discounting most dogmatic slants as the results of zealotry rather than insight. Therefore, 'left or right' (by any other names) has ceased to mean anything to me now. In fact, they become mostly made-up words.

Sometimes it feels as if all the social, cultural, health, public—even personal—issues have been streamlined and polarized with simple labels. This has a tendency to divide society and people.

When our American-born daughter prepares to cook, she lays out all the ingredients, equipment, and measuring cups, covering the entire countertop. She then follows the long recipe as if it were scripture. "In China," I said to her, "cooking involves no recipes."

"But that would be scary. How do I know how it would turn out?" She seemed puzzled.

"People follow their instincts, and use what they have on hand to experiment," I explained. "After some trial-and-error, you will make progress, and eventually create your own recipes."

I suppose we cannot expect the prevailing paradigm of conformity to recede anytime soon, yet we could certainly alter our attitude toward it. Isn't life supposed to be more like art?

As scholar Matthew C. MacWilliams wrote: "Personally, we need to stop 'othering' each other. No more schoolyard labeling…as 'libtard,' 'snowflake,' or 'deplorable.' No more reveling in the drawing of differences between us and them."

Regardless of my apolitical stance, I volunteered to join the Wake County Election Board committee for the 2020 election year. I wanted to get a close-up view of this inspirational land with the highest ideas at heart. Simply casting a vote every four years does not cut it for me. Manning a booth at a polling station in the Auditorium-Gymnasium at Alston Ridge Elementary School in Cary, North Carolina, on Election Day—out my door at 5:00 am until I was back home at 9:00 pm—I think I have witnessed the absolute best of this country firsthand. Voters of all races and ethnicities—ranging from eighteen-year-old students to a ninety-three-year-old black lady with her daughter following from behind—walked up to the booth one by one. Their uniformly hopeful smiles beamed confidence at making a difference in something much larger than themselves. This, I believe, is the best part of America. A collectively optimistic nature and attitude is the best antidote to distrust, alienation, or any extreme "isms." This nation relies on a well-defined system to guide it toward an ever-brighter future.

One morning, I went out to check my mailbox. A letter caught my eye instantly: it was from Mr. Fu, in Beijing—the man who had so kindly helped me with my English test! Inside, it had only one line: "Writing primarily should be for one reader—yourself. If it is good enough for you, which has worked well for me, you then have found the most meaningful gift in life." But when I tried to seek more information from the note, I jolted awake to find myself not gazing at a letter, but at my bedroom ceiling. However, those words have stuck with me ever since. I believe they are what Mr. Fu would have said to me had I kept our rendezvous before I left Beijing.

"My entire life, I have relished writing that conveys so much enjoyment. Having been on the receiving end, I now want to experience what it would be like at the other end—to pour my ideas and emotions out in the form of words. I need to be close to writers, as that is the only way I might become one."

The Triangle Association of Freelancers (TAF) has become my new oasis for creativity. At first, it felt like the most absurd thing I had ever done—and I still feel that way today. How can I, an old-timer and a non-native speaker who has never been trained in English writing, attempt something this large? But a second thought occurred to me: "Is there any other way to do it if this is what you want most?"

This group is comprised of over 200 writers and editors, and many of them are well-established published authors. However, after showing up, I felt like a paralyzed, rogue cell in a colossal organism, whether in person or online. I have never felt so out of place, as though the gulf between us formed an impassable barrier, one far more daunting than the Pacific.

I was never so timid among people. Yet, I had never felt so encouraged and nourished, either. No one told me I was crazy, although the notion has always lingered in my head. Don, the TAF organizer and a revered prolific writer, opened his home to a group of people, including me, to instruct us in nonfiction writing for six weeks. He has always provided sincere recommendations on anything I have sent to him.

Another member, Ed, was like my personal tutor, making suggestions right down to word choice and punctuation on the practice texts I sent to him. Alison wrote back to me more than once: "Keep doing it your own way, in your own voice. You have a unique niche, style, and perspective." And then there is Kyle, Lisa, Joel, among many others...

My most audacious attempt has awakened a lifelong yearning in me. It has led me to reassemble a journey long buried in my half-century of memories, onto these pages to share with the world.

Leaving home to cross half the globe has only led me to another home. I cannot yet close the book on whether intercultural perspectives make a person more worldly. But I praise the saying by Yo-Yo Ma, French-born American cellist and United Nations Messenger of Peace, "Our cultural strength has always been derived from our diversity of understanding and experience."

From a quest seeking a place I can call home to feeling at home on both sides of the Pacific, I feel the positive vibe from Yo-Yo Ma. In any case, I have crossed paths with people of all creeds, races, and origins. I relish heterogeneous cuisines and enjoy the works of original Western and Eastern literature. And that, to me, is plenty. People say one should have a dream. For me, that dream is not about a final product, a place, or a finish line. Instead, I will let my restless and somewhat fearless spirit lead the way.

ACKNOWLEDGMENTS

RECALLING MEMORIES IS AN incredible voyage through time—it is as if I have lived my life twice. Only this time, I'm able to convey gratefulness to the people who, by happenstance or destiny, have entered my life and shaped me into the person I am today.

I have put my best effort to do justice to them all, but errors and omissions are inevitable, and were all mine to make. Furthermore, I have a long list of people I feel immensely grateful to (many are part of my memoir, yet a lot more cannot be mentioned in this confined space). Although they have not directly contributed to reconstructing my journey on paper, they are, in fact, my true inspiration, motivation, and the predominant theme of my storyline.

After the first chapter of this memoir commenced from a random online writing assignment, I began to immerse myself in excavating my recollections. Even then, this newfound inspiration could only be sustained for so long under normal circumstances.

However, the year 2020 was anything but normal. It was a tumultuous year—a global pandemic, hate crimes, and social division that each fed into another in a way that no one had seen coming. The words "exhausting," "lost," and "chaotic" are most often used to describe it.

On the other hand, a life on hiatus due to the pandemic has made me realize that my mind does not always belong to me. It has its own will and legs. When I was forced to stay inside, my mind refused to be walled in and went out on its own, wandering around until it found something to focus on. I was able to channel my thoughts to my past, reliving half a century of my life and pouring my heart into getting my story out in the form of words. "It is not the strongest of the species that survives, nor the most intelligent, but the one most responsive to change." Darwin has proven to be correct in that. Nevertheless, I still consider 2020 as a year to despise, and only hope we all have learned a lesson or two from it!

Through it all, my family remains my solid bedrock, which has done far more for a creative process than people give them credit for. Our close-knit family bond fosters an atmosphere—caring, supportive, unburdened, and engaging—that sustains a state of mind that allows for novel ideas to flow. We don't always live together: Cintty's family settled in Atlanta, and Peiyuan spends more time in Shanghai than North Carolina (while I'm the opposite), but we all communicate daily. Peiyuan is a lifetime biologist, brilliant in science and cohesive amongst people. Our dissimilarities in backgrounds and personalities are more conducive for wide-ranged, lively conversations.

Cintty, an American-born, raised, and educated veterinarian, has read all my previous blog articles and gotten me on track with enough rudimentary English grammar that she believed I could be left on my own when writing. She works and raises our lovely granddaughter with David, her Aerospace Engineering Ph.D. husband. They have handled their careers and family amazingly well. In China, grandparents are supposed to take care of the grandchildren by an unwritten social rule. But in our family, we have never even discussed this—not that this retired grandpa couldn't, shouldn't, or wouldn't do that. As things turned out, a stress-free, accommodating environment has proved to be a perfect ecosystem for getting this inconceivable project completed.

The trust and synergy our family has nurtured allows me to feel as if I am writing for more than myself, with ease and pleasure. However, the textual clarity, logical progression, and overall coherence was another question entirely, which I seriously suspected no matter how many times I had rewritten the book. I began to wonder who I could turn to for a comprehensive assessment. Where could I find that right reviewer for my work, someone who is equally as enthusiastic about another cultural and social phenomena as about the English language convention? And how would I know at first sight? That was when synchronicity came into play.

I have been primarily sedentary on social media, but one author I connected with who was also writing about China mentioned that

Made in the USA
Las Vegas, NV
11 September 2021